# Contents

# Part 1

## Introduction

## The life and times of Philip Larkin

At the time of his death in 1985, Philip Larkin was widely regarded as the most significant poet of post-war Britain. He had published only four volumes of poetry, as well as two early novels and some essays; and the recent editor of his *Collected Poems* has been able to find little other work of substance. Yet the last three of his books of poetry demonstrated very clearly that Larkin was a master of his art: these poems are concise, elegantly and economically descriptive, versatile in their use of forms, endlessly suggestive of deeper resonances in the scenes they paint. Perhaps more than this, it became evident from the reception of his poetry that Larkin was far more than a craftsman: that there was a profound affinity between the characteristic moods and tones of his poetry and the currents of feeling running through Britain itself in the forty years of his writing career.

Larkin was born in Coventry in 1922, and went to the King Henry VIII School there, where, by his own account, he was good at nothing but English, and spent most of his time reading. He went to Oxford in 1940, and there we have evidence of his second major interest aside from poetry: jazz, about which he wrote some memorable pieces of criticism. Among his friends at Oxford were Kingsley Amis and John Wain, both of whom were to exert a strong influence on his early writing. He achieved a first-class degree in 1943, but had no clear idea of a career.

He drifted into a job as librarian at the public library in Wellington, and it was while he was there, in 1945, that he produced his first volume of poetry, *The North Ship*. His influences then clearly included W. B. Yeats and Dylan Thomas; and although *The North Ship* included some good poems, and even more good phrases, it gave little hint as to where his poetry was to take him. In 1946 he published a novel, *Jill*, which was to a considerable extent based on his experiences in war-time Oxford; and this was followed in 1947 by a second novel, *A Girl in Winter*.

By this time Larkin was working in the library at Leicester University, where he remained until 1950, when he moved to a similar but superior job at Queen's University, Belfast. It was at this point in the early 1950s that he began to develop the poetic style which we now associate with him; and these were, by Larkin's standards, prolific years, culminating in the publication in 1955 of the collection *The Less Deceived*. Some of his work was also included in two very important anthologies of the period, *Poets of the 1950s* edited by D. J. Enright in 1950, and *New Lines* edited by Robert Conquest in 1956.

The significance of these anthologies lay in the fact that, between them, they amounted to a manifesto for a group of British poets known simply as 'The Movement', and Larkin's work was seen as central to this poetic tendency. Basically, the Movement formed its ideas in reaction to previous movements in British poetry. Where T. S. Eliot and the modernists of the 1920s had preached the value of difficulty and had opened themselves to new influences from the past tradition in English literature and from European and American writing, the Movement stood for simplicity and even colloquialism of expression and adopted firmly British values and forms. Where W. H. Auden and the political poets of the 1930s exalted the social role of the poet and the necessity of political change, the Movement returned to the everyday and to a poetry firmly divorced from political programmes. Where Dylan Thomas and the 'New Apocalyptics' of the 1940s spoke of the intensity of their emotions and the consequent dislocation of ordinary syntax, the Movement prided itself on keeping the emotions under firm control and tended to regard poetry as one part of the everyday communication of one person to others.

On the positive side, the Movement was concerned with economy of expression and with tightness of verse form; and these are very much skills in tune with Larkin's genius. Although he chose to make very few public pronouncements on his writing, most of them concentrated on the need for a poetry which moves beyond an 'initiated' audience and can find some kind of resonance with common experience. There is a certain irony here, since by far the majority of Movement poets were academics and many of them were, or became, substantial critics in their own right; but the Movement still stood for a separation of poetic and academic activity, and laid claim to a broad audience for poetry, a claim which, not surprisingly, it found hard to acquit.

*The Less Deceived* was a considerable success, and was reprinted three times during the year after its first publication. At this time, Larkin moved from Northern Ireland to take the position of librarian of the university library at Hull, a position which he held until his death. His third volume of poems, *The Whitsun Weddings*, was published in 1964, and consolidated his reputation as one of Britain's

# YORK NOTES

*General Editors:* Professor A.N. Jeffares (*University of Stirling*) & Professor Suheil Bushrui (*American University of Beirut*)

Philip Larkin

# SELECTED POEMS

*Notes by David Punter*

Professor of English Studies,
University of Stirling

LONGMAN
YORK PRESS

YORK PRESS
Immeuble Esseily, Place Riad Solh, Beirut

LONGMAN GROUP LIMITED
*Longman House, Burnt Mill, Harlow,*
*Essex CM20 2JE, England*
*Associated companies, branches and representatives*
*throughout the world*

First published 1991
Sixth impression 1995

ISBN 0-582-06564-X

Produced by Longman Singapore Publishers Pte Ltd
Printed in Singapore

foremost poets; he was awarded the Queen's Gold Medal for Poetry in 1965. His fourth and final volume, *High Windows*, appeared in 1974. On the death of the then poet laureate, Sir John Betjeman, in 1984, it was widely rumoured that Larkin would be his successor; and although the reasons for this not happening have never been made fully public, it seems likely that only increasing ill-health and a lifelong habit of seclusion were responsible. Certainly by that time he was Britain's best-known poet, and one of the most quoted.

Larkin's poetic career thus spans enormous changes in British society, from the war through to the 1970s; but we find quite few poems of his which refer directly to historical or social events. The influence of British social life on his work, while enormously strong, has to be seen in broader terms than that. For Larkin always had an impressive knowledge of ordinary life as it is lived by millions of British people. He is familiar with the high street shops; he is familiar with the weather; he is familiar with the maxims and sayings by which people actually govern their lives. In other words, he prefers to describe life as it is lived rather than to measure life by unattainable ideals.

Much can be gained by comparing Larkin's poetic environment with that of his nearest rival to poetic fame over the last forty years, Ted Hughes, who took the laureateship in 1984. Hughes is a poet of the vast distances: most of his poetry is set in rural surroundings, or in the grinding daily life of people who are themselves remote from society. Larkin always preferred to look at more common lives, lives in suburbia, lives in small towns. Where Hughes tends to look for transcendental meanings and to find these by contrasting the inadequacies of human life with the instinctual harmonies of the animal kingdom, Larkin remained content to extract meanings painstakingly from the rituals and ceremonies with which we attempt to surround and protect lives which might otherwise be thoroughly debased.

For all that, as we read through his poetry we can sense the movements of history. His first novel, *Jill*, has often been compared with the novels of the Angry Young Men: John Braine, Allan Sillitoe and others; and while that is not a very happy connection, it is true that Larkin transparently belongs to a generation who hoped for much after the war, and were disappointed.

But disappointment did not make Larkin angry; or rather, anger is not one of the moods frequently reflected in his poetry. It contributes rather to a strong but gentle irony: a sense that any ideal exists only to be betrayed, and therefore perhaps it is better not to have ideals at all. But even that makes Larkin's poetry sound too prescriptive: for Larkin does not try to teach us how to live, rather he shows us some of the accommodations he made with the problems of living and some of the accommodations other people make, and invites his readers to inspect them.

British society, of course, went through a major upheaval in the 1960s. The painful austerity of the immediate post-war years – made all the more painful by the contemporary hopes for a rapid transformation and opening-up of a stagnant society, hopes which although not entirely dashed were never met in full measure – gave way to a sudden affluence, and a sense that therefore many of the restrictions of an older way of life were no longer necessary. These were the years of the 'generation gap', years when the young went into wholesale revolt against received wisdom; and in several of his poems of the period Larkin reflects ruefully on the attraction of this sense of hope, although always from the position of a man already too old and too set in his ways fully to benefit from it.

As time has passed on, the sense of imminent change that prevailed throughout the 1960s has been increasingly replaced by a new awareness of constraint: the real economic constraint which must operate in a country which is no longer as powerful as it once was, and the wider constraint to do with how we can manage with a world of diminishing natural resources. It seems fair to say that, as British society has turned full circle back to the rigours of a rationed economy – even if not as literally rationed as in the 1950s – we have, so to speak, Larkin waiting for us. For he was never carried away on the wave of optimism; there remained throughout his poetry a sense that any success, any achievement, has to be paid for, especially in a society in which freedom is less natural than an unthinking obedience to the power of tradition.

Yet for all the emphasis on ordinariness, it could be argued that Larkin's life was, after all, extraordinary in the most obvious ways: he was a lifelong bachelor, and a man apparently wary of deep personal relationships. In a lesser poet this might well have limited his field of human sympathy; it is an extraordinary feature of Larkin's writing that he is able to deploy his outsider status wittily, ironically, and to the advantage of his reader as he ceaselessly compares his own situation with the situations of those he sees around him.

He actually has a very strong sense of the generations: of siblings, of fathers and sons, of the intricacies of the family. Often the family does serve as a site for claustrophobia: yet in a Larkin poem we can rarely be free from ambiguities in this area, as Larkin on the one hand appears to relish his freedom from ties, while on the other he suggests the real human warmth which the family can (if only occasionally) provide. The emotions which Larkin seems to wish to conjure up are always *tempered* ones: satisfaction tinged with regret, mournfulness tinged with hope, despair about communication tinged with a curious elation about being free.

Isolating the literary influences at work on Larkin's poetry is not simple. Clearly the early influences of symbolism, through Yeats and Thomas, waned, although they never disappeared entirely. Whether Larkin was ever *influenced* by the Movement is harder to say; perhaps the best way of putting it is that the Movement was a group of people working under similar influences, which induced in them a particular kind of realism in their attitudes to life. We might then fairly say that Larkin stayed within that ambit throughout his writing life, and certainly modernist and post-modernist developments in literature had little visible effect on his style.

The great influence claimed by the Movement was the poetry of Thomas Hardy, and here one can see a useful comparison, for Larkin was always concerned with the traditional rhythms of English poetry, with the everyday scenes and sights of English life. But all of this seems less than conscious in Larkin: less as though he is making a choice than as though his thoughts and feelings are naturally attuned to the standard English verse-forms.

Also, Larkin's poetry is much more acerbic than Hardy's, and can be very terse indeed. In a good number of his poems he seems deliberately to disown elegance and accuracy of language and to opt instead for the debased language of contemporary usage. He is famous, for example, for his use of swearwords. But in this he is not totally at odds with Hardy, because, of course, the occasionally scurrilous tone of Larkin's language might fairly be considered as parallel to Hardy's usage of the social decencies of his own time.

In the end, it has to be said that Larkin was a poet under nobody's influence. One of his great strengths is his almost unthinking alertness to contemporary conversational tones and rhythms; he never pontificates, and he never settles for the easy answer. His problem, perhaps – and it might in part account for the slightness of his output – lay in finding those moments when colloquial thought, feeling and language can come together in an unstrained way with the drive for formality which structures his poems. When he achieves this, it is a testimony not only to his own poetic power and prodigious reading but also to the ear for a poetic phrase which is, one should say, not the province of the poet alone. For after all, there is great poetic skill in old sayings, proverbs, in people's everyday ways of putting things; it is this unthought skill which Larkin is able to tune into and raise to another notch without sacrificing the common applicability of age-old truths.

We might say, then, that Larkin's life had a shape which was eccentric – in his singleness, in his job, in his improbable background for a poet – and yet emblematic, in so far as he shared many of the frustrations and difficulties of people of his generation; and it is this conjunction of marginality and common understanding which lies behind the greatness of his poetry – as, perhaps, it lay behind Shakespeare's.

In one of the most splendid of his poems, 'An Arundel Tomb', Larkin describes the dignity of death, but is unable to prevent himself from mentioning a 'faint hint of the absurd' in the whole business of surviving, in any form, after one has gone. This sense of the necessity of preservation, combined with the ridiculousness of assigning to any individual human life more than is its due is intrinsic to his poetry; and so perhaps Larkin himself had more to say on the nature of biography than any future commentator can ever have.

# A note on the text

With a poet as careful as Larkin, there are no obvious problems with the text. These Notes are based on Philip Larkin, *Collected Poems*, edited with an Introduction by Anthony Thwaite (Faber and Faber, 1988), which contains all of Larkin's published poems, with a selection of juvenilia. In the Summaries that follow, poems are discussed in the order in which they appear in this volume. Larkin's four principal collections, *The North Ship* (1945), *The Less Deceived* (1955), *The Whitsun Weddings* (1964) and *High Windows* (1974) are obvious primary sources, and it is useful to consult them, because one can thereby gain a sense of the shape of each volume; but textually there are no discrepancies between these and the poems as reproduced in Thwaite's edition.

# Part 2

# Summaries
*of* SELECTED POEMS

---

**'Wedding-Wind'** from *The Less Deceived*

---

The persona of this poem is a woman: a young woman, a farm girl perhaps. It is the day after her wedding; in the first verse paragraph she takes us back to her wedding-day and wedding-night, and to her new husband. Very gently in this paragraph we are introduced to her happiness and sense of fulfilment at being married and her sense of loss when her new husband is absent even for a short time. When she thinks about the horses, restless because of the wind, it is only to contrast that restlessness with her own peace and contentment.

In the second paragraph, on the surface all is back to normal again; there are the effects of the rain to be dealt with, the chickens to be fed. But in the midst of this normality the wind encourages in her a reverie in which she listens in her mind to the wind and thinks of it as a force which is comparable to the all-changing joy she feels. Although there is peace, there is also the underlying feeling that everything has altered, that her new condition is so filled with joy that it seems as though it might transcend death itself. At the end she offers up a kind of hymn of praise to the powers which have allowed her this life-altering experience, an experience which, she feels, will never leave her.

COMMENTARY:
Larkin takes great care to introduce us to the simplicity of this girl: the phrase "That he must go and shut it' is slightly colloquial; the phrase 'I was sad' moves by its clarity and the directness of feeling it expresses.

At the same time, the imagery itself is not simple. The central image of the wind might perhaps remind us of the wind which 'long has raved unnoticed' in Coleridge's 'Dejection: An Ode', or of Shelley's 'Ode to the West Wind'. It goes through three distinct stages. In the first paragraph we are invited to experience the wind literally and its power to disturb yet also to reassure her in her secure happiness, which she wishes all creatures to share. Her reverie starts with 'All is the wind', reminding us that the wind is a greater and

wider power than that of the merely human. In the end we are all at
the mercy of the wind, although in her case the wind is indeed
merciful.

The most complex part of the image is in the lines:

> Can it be borne, this bodying-forth by wind
> Of joy my actions turn on, like a thread
> Carrying beads?

Might the wind, Larkin asks, be too strong for us? Or might we see it
as a unifying force, as something which makes sense of all our
actions, even if we cannot ourselves understand them? And there is
also a hint of the beads of the rosary, which moves us on to the
'thanksgiving' mood of the final lines.

Those final lines are biblical in their feel, but not insistently so; we
are invited to think about the simple religion which this girl has
absorbed, which is compounded of Christianity and an older, nature-
based sense of awe. The world of Thomas Hardy, always a
formidable influence on English poetry in this century, can be sensed
throughout.

For all the sense of peace, there is also an undertone of disturbance
in the poem. The girl's happiness reminds her of the frailty of the
human; it is as though in her simplicity she is content to resign herself
to a higher power, trusting and pliant, and to see herself as akin to the
'cattle'. Yet for all that she cannot see the future clearly; she is too
much under the spell of this almost magical process of transformation
to know what will come next. The word 'thrashing' and the phrase
'Shall I be let to sleep' remind us that powers which can seem to be
beneficial also constitute an exposure to forces immeasurably greater
than ourselves; and who can know what the consequences of this may
be?

NOTES AND GLOSSARY:

**ravelled:** one of the rare words in the English language which also means its own opposite: 'entangled' and 'disentangled'

**bodying-forth:** giving a shape to, incarnating

---

## 'Days' from *The Whitsun Weddings*

---

This poem takes a very simple word, and a very simple notion,
'days' – one which, perhaps, we never ordinarily think about at
all – and inspects it. No story is told here, and we have no characters
to connect with; instead we have a brief contemplation and one
which, at first glance, may seem deeply inconclusive.

COMMENTARY:
This very short poem, which uses extremely simple language, nevertheless demonstrates, as we look at it carefully, considerable skill and also an interesting approach to vital matters of life and death. It is a good poem on which to attempt a line-by-line analysis.

'What are days for?' The question sounds childlike; we almost expect 'mummy' to appear at the end of the line, as if the question itself could only be put by somebody to whom the very word 'days' is new – a child who, for example, has just come across it for the first time in an alphabet book.

'Days are where we live'. The concept here is one of home, of homeliness, of feeling at home in the world. In the brightness of daylight we feel that we can understand things, that a straight-forward, clear account of the world makes sense. Already perhaps we can hear the other, unasked question: what, then, of nights? If days are the source of our reassurance of life, what then of darkness, of that which we cannot understand?

'They come, they wake us'. We sense here a possible reply by the parent to the child. Of course we know that it is not precisely the case that 'days' wake us; but this answer, the poet implies, will perhaps suffice for the child, for somebody to whom the whole world is still a mystery to be enjoyed.

'Time and time over'. This line contains an ambiguity. On the surface it means the same as 'Time and time again'; but the separate phrase 'time over' carries an implication of the end of this safe world of days without end.

'They are to be happy in'. Again the tone of the parent answering the child; and perhaps by this time we may sense that this is a drama of question and answer which is also being enacted *within* an individual – the reader, for example – in which the innocence of the questioning represents a desire to be satisfied by simplicity, although the happiness spoken of may in fact prove elusive.

'Where can we live but days?' This line moves us on from the question-and-answer format, as though the voice of the parent is now asking itself a question. As we reassure our children of life, light, happiness, perhaps we also ask ourselves what is the 'other side' of days.

The break between the two stanzas marks a change: a change of mood from certainty to puzzlement, and also a change of versification such that the simple monosyllables which signify an unchanging world are replaced by two-syllable words like 'question', 'doctor', 'running', which increase the urgency of the poem and suggest to us the deeper problems of time which cannot be answered by just referring to life as consisting of an endless succession of days.

'Ah, solving that question'. The initial 'Ah' also marks this break; rather than briskly answering questions, the poetic voice is now moving further into reverie. 'Solving', as well as meaning 'finding a solution to', carries a hint of 'dissolving', so that we see that the wider questions require us to dissolve the apparent certainties of the first stanza.

'Brings the priest and the doctor'. Why the priest and the doctor? They are the people who are concerned with the real problems of mortality: with the health and survival of the soul, with the health of the body; in short, with death.

'In their long coats'. This is, of course, a literal reference to the priest's cassock, to the doctor's white coat. But we sense in these 'long coats' also the force of a symbol, although, like all symbols, it may be difficult to pin down. We are here being referred back to the world of the child, but now in a frightening way: to the sense a child may have that somebody in a 'long coat' may represent problems beyond control, beyond understanding.

'Running over the fields'. The fields are the bright, sunlit fields of day; the priest and the doctor spoil this perfect picture, and they also bring into a peaceful scene a note of urgency, the urgency which follows from our gradual recognition – enacted throughout the poem – of the superior power of death, the decay of the body, and the need to find an answer, beyond the grave, to the initial questions and particularly to the question which occurs around the midpoint of the poem, 'Where can we live but days?' When days run out, shall we find ourselves still living? And in what way?

---

## 'Toads' from *The Less Deceived*

As in other poems, Larkin here takes on the persona of the common man, asking questions about things which we take for granted. We might assume that life consists mainly of working, in this case six days a week – or perhaps the sixth day is spent worrying about work! But why should this be the case? Might there not be a better way to live?

The persona sees other people, people on the fringes of society, living without this compulsion to work: gypsies, academics – by implication, perhaps, poets. By living in this way people do not get rich, but they survive.

But how, he asks, can he get himself into this position? So many of us are bound into our jobs, our habits of life. We fear for the future; we fear what will happen to us if at the end of the day we do not have a pension on which to fall back.

We must conclude, then, that this compulsion to work, to conform to the norms of society, is not merely something imposed from the outside, something which squats like a toad on our deeper wishes for freedom, unconventionality; instead it is something which lives inside ourselves, something which we have *internalised*; it 'squats in me, too'. It is nonetheless perceived as inevitable; the fear embodied in 'hard luck' and the coldness of 'snow' represent the internal pressures which keep us from any attempt to break free.

There may be *other* people who can gratify their desires, get 'the fame and the girl and the money' without working; but we can never be like them. What we are left with instead is the perpetual compromise embodied in the last stanza, for although Larkin seems positive at this point – 'when you have both' – we are invited to see an irony here, a way in which we all persuade ourselves, after all, that the conventional lives we lead are more satisfying and less risky than the other lives which, from time to time, we may find ourselves envying.

COMMENTARY:
The poem is called 'Toads', not 'Toad'; and so it cannot refer only to the 'toad *work*' but must also refer to the way in which we ourselves become toadlike, unimaginative, weighed down by our bodies and by habit as we submit to these pressures.

The stanza form Larkin uses is jaunty, almost throwaway; it suggests an absence of deep thought, and this is because Larkin is here talking about the excuses we offer to ourselves to avoid thinking deeply about our situation. Although the persona may appear to value the lives of those outside the social pale, the terms he uses of them – 'lispers,/Losels, loblolly-men, louts' – simultaneously suggest that he avoids considering them as serious alternatives by despising them.

The word 'wit'/'wits' in stanzas one and three implicitly compares the 'wit' of the poet, or simply of the intelligent person, with the 'wits' of the person who has the perhaps innate skills to avoid the toad; but the comparison is ironic, so that in the end the poem appears to try to persuade us that real 'wit' or intelligence can only end up making us content with the way things are.

Notice the sudden changes of tone: for example, the language of 'pitchfork', 'brute', 'sickening', contrasted with the colloquialism of 'Just for paying a few bills'. From the beginning we are unsettled as to how seriously we should take the argument being advanced. The irony here is all-pervasive; we are invited to consider the opinion of the persona as representing a serious alternative while we can see that he is in fact prejudiced and timid.

Notice also the contempt in the fifth stanza: 'Their unspeakable wives/Are skinny as whippets'. This persona is one who really scorns those who are beyond convention, and therefore it is not surprising that he cannot move beyond convention himself.

There is a considerable change of tone at the beginning of the seventh stanza, where we are made to feel the real sombreness of a life lived according to the dictates of the toad. But this moment of revelation and fear cannot be sustained by the persona, who needs to cheer himself up in the joking tones of stanza eight.

What, then, does the last stanza mean? Perhaps there is no definitive answer to this, but we could say that the 'one' and the 'other' are the two types of life being talked about, in which case the persona is concluding by saying that he has both of these kinds of life. But surely if this is true, then he only has the second kind of life, the life of 'toadlessness', *in his imagination*; and if that is true, does that make him timid, or self-deluding, or is he finally talking about the unavoidable ambiguity of being a poet, whose business it is to imagine but not to live out other people's lives?

NOTES AND GLOSSARY:

| | |
|---|---|
| **lispers:** | Larkin here implies homosexuals and poets in the same term, on the assumption that this bracketing is familiar to the presumed 'common man' |
| **losels:** | (*archaic*) rascals |
| **loblolly-men:** | a dialect word for louts |
| **windfalls:** | fruit blown down by the wind; but also unexpected good luck |
| **whippets:** | extraordinarily thin racing dogs |
| **the stuff/That dreams are made on:** | a virtual quotation from Shakespeare, *The Tempest* IV.1.156–7 |
| **hunkers:** | haunches |
| **blarney:** | an Irish word for cajole |

---

## 'Church Going' from *The Less Deceived*

---

This is one of Larkin's most famous and complex poems, and in it he again assumes the persona of the common man trying to explain to himself some of the most commanding features of British culture, in this case the meaning of religious observance.

We are to picture him as a casual weekend cyclist who arrives at a church. In the first two stanzas he enters the church, not knowing quite how to behave; he knows that people remove their hats in churches, but since he has no hat he removes his cycle-clips instead. He can see the significant features of the building, knows which end is which, but he does not have the knowledge or the sensibility to enter deeply into this. Instead he does the things any tourist might do, and leaves none the wiser.

Or so it seems. But in the third stanza we are told that this is not just a single event, that he has often felt compelled to visit churches in this way before. He begins to meditate, as before, on what use churches are now that established Christianity is in decay. Will churches become – or have they already become – museums whose real purpose is lost? Or will they, as he suggests in stanza four, become the haunt of latter-day witches? What strange people, he asks in stanza five, will eventually remain interested in churches, and how distant will their motives be from those which inspired the religion to which they were originally dedicated?

In stanza six he returns to his apparently uninformed stance, yet also suggests that, at least, the ceremonies of life, marriage and death retain, whether we know it or not, their overarching importance as markers of our lives. And in the final stanza he changes tone markedly, to recognise in highly serious language that, after all, no matter how decayed a church or religion itself may be, nevertheless it remains a kind of magnet for the more serious, profound aspects of our feelings, feelings which will never die and which may continue to need for their proper expression a 'serious house on serious earth', no matter how far our personal motives and capacities may have diverged from the original intent of the Church.

COMMENTARY:
In stanza three Larkin uses the phrase 'parchment, plate and pyx'. We might fairly ask: if he really is the common man of the persona, then how would he know about such erudite terms? This opens up the whole question of the relation between Larkin and his persona: to what extent is he adopting a pose of learning but ironically suggesting that the era in which learning is valued is at an end?

The poem is written in seven nine-line stanzas, with a very regular form. The typical line is an iambic pentameter; by using this line Larkin asserts his sense of continuity with many other English poets, for this is the most frequent line form in English-language poetry. Notice the rhyme scheme: we may formally describe it as ABABCADCD, but we also encounter within this structure many half-rhymes: that is, rhymes where the consonants match but the vowels although related are not identical: 'on'/'stone', 'stuff'/'off', and so forth.

Notice also how ably Larkin uses this complex versification to contain sentences of ordinary, even colloquial, syntax: for example, 'Someone would know: I don't'. In this way he manages to convey a *double* voice, the voice of the ordinary man, reflected in the sentence structure, alongside or set off against the voice of the poet, reflected in the verse form, in the rhyme and rhythm.

At the beginning of the fourth stanza Larkin elevates and mystifies his language. Why does he do this? He suggests, first, the connection of the church with a cultural tradition; second, the poet's own access to such tradition; third, the way in which such tradition can appear in the contemporary world only in debased form; fourth, the way in which even an apparently uneducated persona when in search of explanations or symbols may inevitably turn to the past as a vehicle for myths, cultural values, the very language which we use in everyday speech.

The title 'Church Going' is ambiguous. It suggests the habit of going to church on Sundays, and it also suggests that the Church itself as an institution is 'going', both in the sense of vanishing and also in the sense that it is perhaps only the church which now marks our own 'going', our passing away.

Consider, as one small emblem of the technique Larkin uses, the phrase 'accoutred frowsty barn'. The words 'accoutred' and 'frowsty barn' almost match in terms of sound, but they come from quite different registers of discourse, the first sounding heraldic, armorial, to do with the past, the second summing up a casual modern judgment. This poem is about the difference between these two registers, and about the way the individual consciousness can be aware of this difference, but also, in the presence of the church and perhaps thus in the presence of God, span it.

NOTES AND GLOSSARY:

| | |
|---|---|
| **font:** | vessel for baptism |
| **lectern:** | desk from which the Bible is read |
| **Irish sixpence:** | Irish coinage is not accepted in the UK (though UK coinage is accepted in the Republic of Ireland); hence it is symbolic of worthless money |
| **pyx:** | container for the communion wafer |
| **dubious:** | here means 'of dubious origin' and 'for dubious purposes' |
| **simples:** | herbal remedies |
| **advised:** | notice that this needs to be given three syllables |
| **rood-lofts:** | gallery over the screen at the entrance to the part of the church containing the altar |
| **ruin-bibber:** | Larkin's own term for somebody who samples ruins for their savour, like wine |
| **randy:** | this word ironically likens the taste for ruins to a taste for sex |
| **gown-and-bands:** | refers to clerical dress |

| myrrh: | perfume carried by one of the three wise men at the Nativity |
| accoutred: | decorated |
| frowsty: | fusty, musty |
| blent: | an archaic version of blended |

---

## 'Mr Bleaney' from *The Whitsun Weddings*

---

We have to picture as the persona of this poem a man who is looking for accommodation. In the opening stanza we hear his potential landlady describing to him the previous occupant of the room to let, Mr Bleaney. The room is unpleasant: cheap and not cared for. But the protagonist finds himself entering in his imagination into the life that Bleaney might have led here.

Clearly the landlady thought highly of him, and they got on all right together despite the lack of amenities in the room. The protagonist decides to rent the room, and finds himself increasingly involved with Bleaney, wondering about his life: he is forced to hear the wireless set which – he supposes – Bleaney persuaded the landlady to buy; he claims in the fifth stanza that he has come to know all about Bleaney, his leisure habits, his family.

But, as is so frequently the case in Larkin's poems, in the sixth stanza we find ourselves invited to an abrupt change of mood. The commonplaces of the first part of the poem become a springboard for a meditation on life and death, and specifically on the importance of the individual to the general course of the world. We are invited to wonder whether Bleaney – whoever he was – had been contented with this bleak (the word is apposite) room; or whether he had glimpsed that even to live in such a room betrayed one's own worthlessness. If the latter is the case, then of course implicitly the poet, who is Bleaney's successor in this same room, is finding himself asking the same questions of himself; and are they questions about some particular temporary room, or about life envisaged *as* a bedsit?

COMMENTARY:
'At the Bodies', whatever it may mean literally, means metaphorically 'in a body' and thus introduces us to the notion that Bleaney's tenancy of the room is akin to our tenancy of the physical. The 'they' of 'They moved him' can thus be nothing but death.

The contrast between the chaos of the curtains which do not fit, the 'tussocky' land outside, and the landlady's claim that Bleaney 'took/My bit of garden properly in hand' is stark: what does it mean to cultivate some small strip when all around is chaos, death and despair?

Notice that in the passages descriptive of the room Larkin omits the definite and the indefinite article: 'Bed, upright chair, sixty-watt bulb'; the effect of this is to generalise this room as a site for life, to claim that we might all end up in this kind of place, a place which is available all over the world.

'Fags' and 'saucer-souvenir' are redolent of a lower-class world. Larkin is certainly saying that Bleaney and his landlady belong to this world; whether he is also saying that he is himself of this world or whether he is saying that such a world permanently threatens him are questions we are left to speculate on.

All through the fifth stanza there runs the parlance of the lower classes – it is not clear whether we are talking here about the working class or the lower middle class; perhaps Mr Bleaney was a travelling salesman – in 'the four aways', an allusion to the football pools; in Frinton and Stoke, which summarise the notoriously unfashionable.

The 'yearly frame', however, deliberately betrays the poet 'framing' this unremarkable life which he is . . . reinventing? inventing? remembering? Perhaps we are here in the presence of the protagonist's own past, a past which he has tried to throw off through education, for example, but to which he finds himself in imagination perpetually returning.

The last stanzas stand in syntactic relation to the 'I know' of stanza four; for this is all that the protagonist does not 'know'. What he does not know is the level of Bleaney's self-awareness. What the poet sees is the waste, the triviality of Bleaney's life; what he does not know is whether Bleaney himself was aware of this. To the poet this room is redolent of death, as well it might be, since Bleaney's life effectively ended here. But did Bleaney himself appreciate the dreadful end to which life had brought him? Did he grin and shiver, like a skeleton, knowing that this final condition of his was the true measure of his worth? And if he did, does this imply that we too should understand that the insufficiencies of our environment, the 'hired box' in which we perhaps live, is a true and just reward for our insufficiency as human beings?

NOTES AND GLOSSARY:

| | |
|---|---|
| **tussocky:** | unkempt |
| **fags:** | colloquial term for cigarettes |
| **jabbering set:** | a radio which, to the poet, makes no sense because he hears it only as background noise |
| **hired box:** | here means a rented room, but with connotations of a horse-box, and consequently of being manipulated without understanding where one is going |

## 'An Arundel Tomb' from *The Whitsun Weddings*

This poem is unusual for Larkin. Although there are lyrical moments in many others of his poems, they are usually undercut by an all-pervading irony; but here the lyrical note, the celebration of past lives, is allowed to stand for itself.

We are looking at a medieval tomb; on that tomb lie the sculptured effigies of the 'earl and countess'. These effigies are weathered by the centuries such that their faces are 'blurred', but the observing eye, playing over this 'vagueness', lights upon the still vivid detail of their hands still clasped in each other's.

The poet enters a reverie, wondering whether this detail, which now appears to him so important, might have been of little significance when they commissioned – before their deaths – the anonymous sculptor to produce their monument. To them and to the sculptor perhaps this detail was merely a triviality compared with the perceived importance of preserving their names, their family's honour.

They would probably have imagined, the poet says in the fourth stanza, that it was their name which would carry continuing importance; instead, he suggests, it is this slight 'grace' of art which is now the only source of interest. The 'tenantry' have gone away; in other words the old feudal certainties on which the earl and countess no doubt based their lives, and also their hopes for remembrance after death, have now vanished, and all that remains of interest is the beauty of their posture – we care 'To look, not read'.

And so 'Time has transfigured them into/Untruth', in the sense that the meanings which their lives and deaths carried have been changed by the further passage of time. We do not know whether the earl and countess were or were not an especially faithful or admirable couple, but the accident by which time has failed to erode their clasped hands nonetheless means that we, the later generations, can still find in them if we choose an emblem for lasting love; but at the same time we need to bear in mind that the reasons why this emblem persists are themselves at the mercy of time, as indeed is love itself.

COMMENTARY:

The stanza structure here is simple and almost architectural in its sturdiness, thereby exemplifying the persistence of the tombs themselves. In itself it symbolises the strength by which art survives the erosion of time.

The mention of the 'absurd' in the first stanza is a characteristic Larkin semi-evasion of the profundity of what he is saying; but the 'sharp tender shock' of the second stanza reverses the flow of this irony, reminding us that no matter how thick our skins may seem to be we can still be touched and moved by the accidental.

In stanza three we encounter some of the many effects Larkin produces through alliteration: there are the 'f' sounds of 'faithfulness in effigy', and more obviously the sliding, continuing sounds of the 's' in 'sweet commissioned grace', which will later be echoed in 'supine stationary voyage'. All of this is a reminder of sleep, the soporific, yet thereby underlines the unconscious means by which survival occurs.

Notice that in the fifth stanza, where Larkin is beginning to talk about the centuries, the changes which have occurred between the lifetimes of the earl and countess and our own age, the stanza itself is broken up, like history perhaps, or like a ploughed field. The smoothness which has earlier in the poem replicated the smooth, sinuous lines of the prone effigies is now replaced by the broken, jagged shapes of verse lines which do not conform to sentence structure:

> Rigidly they
>
> Persisted, linked, through lengths and breadths
> Of time. Snow fell, undated. Light
> Each summer thronged the glass. A bright
> Litter of birdcalls strewed the same
> Bone-riddled ground.

In the very form of the verse Larkin is questioning this 'rigidity': are these feudal forms genuinely surviving, or do they lie athwart history? Do these effigies represent something we can still find operative in our daily lives, or are they a heritage which we have to break up, to overcome?

The 'endless altered people' (the pun on 'altar' is intended, because there are hints of an act of worship here) represent a different truth, but not necessarily a better one. The 'trough/Of smoke in slow suspended skeins' reminds us of that supreme image of death and the glory of mortality, the seventeenth-century poet John Donne's 'bracelet of bright hair about the bone'.

What then are 'untruth' and 'fidelity'? Evidence, perhaps, that love is all-conquering; but we can only half-believe this, perhaps because of the age in which we live, perhaps because we are ourselves, as were the earl and the countess, proudly and humiliatingly mortal.

NOTES AND GLOSSARY:
**little dogs under their feet:** conventional tomb trappings of a knight
**pre-baroque:** here refers to an artistic period before excessive

| | embellishment, a time when clear lines, artistic, moral and social, could be picked out |
| unarmorial: | here, 'without real distinction', in all senses |
| skeins: | loosely tied lengths of thread |
| blazon: | coat-of-arms; here, evidence that they lived |

---

**'The Whitsun Weddings'** from *The Whitsun Weddings*

---

This is the best-known of Larkin's poems. The persona is on a train journey. The train is slow; the whole mood is unhurried, and Larkin brings alive for us the unremarkable sights one encounters on any provincial train journey.

He has not intended to travel at Whitsun; indeed, we realise that he has no associations with Whitsun as a ceremony. Therefore in stanza three we learn that he is not looking out for evidence of the popularity – a time-honoured popularity – of Whitsun as an auspicious time for marriages.

As the train moves through station after station he begins to realise that the sounds he is hearing cannot simply be 'porters larking with the mails', and he notices at last that, on every station, there are families seeing bride and bridegroom off on their honeymoons.

'Each face seemed to define/Just what it saw departing'; in other words the persona is brought face to face with this evidence of people trusting in new beginings, but he cannot see it quite as that; instead, he sees marriage more as a continuation of the failings of the past, the 'uncle shouting smut'. He glimpses something significant here – 'Free at last' – but refers it back to the inescapability of convention – 'shuffling gouts of steam'.

In the final stanza, however, we are confronted by a crucial image which seems to cast doubt on the persona's smug refusal of change: 'there swelled/A sense of falling, like an arrow-shower/Sent out of sight, somewhere becoming rain'. It is as though Larkin is saying that although these weddings, these acts of trust, repeated in the face of the continual disillusionment offered by life might be considered as mere acts of conventional piety, he nonetheless recognises that, really, he cannot know the outcome of them or is unable really to feel the oft-repeated hope they represent; who is to deny that somewhere, somehow, these hopes might be fulfilled?

COMMENTARY:
This poem demonstrates a problem in Larkin's poetry in general: what is the relation between the ironic and the non-ironic perception? For example, in the fourth stanza he portrays the families of the newly-weds in highly unflattering terms:

The fathers with broad belts under their suits
And seamy foreheads; mothers loud and fat;
An uncle shouting smut; and then the perms,
The nylon gloves and jewellery-substitutes,
The lemons, mauves, and olive-ochres . . .

But whose is this perception? Is it Larkin's, or that of his persona? Does Larkin mean us to accept this as an unchallengeable portrayal of a certain class, or does he offer it to us as evidence of social prejudice?

He treads a thin line here, but saves himself by an unblemished accuracy of description. We can find it, for example, in the famous lines about 'London spread out in the sun,/Its postal districts packed like squares of wheat': here Larkin reaches for an image which conjoins London as a place *seen* and as a place *imagined from maps* (as it would be to the wedding parties) and, superbly, finds it.

There are dozens of images in this poem which demonstrate that extraordinary mastery: 'a street/Of blinding windscreens', 'the reek of buttoned carriage-cloth', 'bright knots of rail'. In all of them Larkin manages to conjoin a *participatory* perception with the observation of a stranger. He is both part of these scenes and aside from, alienated from them. His persona, we might say, is fatally implicated in this world of perms and nylon gloves, yet is also ceaselessly aware of his distance from a society which, for all its gaucheness and grotesquerie, might yet be the only one which could save him from his isolation.

This poem is as much about the protagonist's isolation, his willed rejection of what he perceives, as it is about the Whitsun weddings themselves. The weddings stand as a double image: of that which one rejects on aesthetic grounds, and also as that which one envies because it provides evidence of a living, if debased, community.

'The Whitsun Weddings' is thus an emblematic poem of the ambiguity of 'community': does belonging to a community involve one in being a self which one does not want to be, or does it remind one of the possibility that one might be rescued from the isolation which is here symbolised by the solitary train journey, on which one can see others only through impermeable windows?

NOTES AND GLOSSARY:

| | |
|---|---|
| **Whitsun:** | the seventh Sunday after Easter, also known as Pentecost, celebrated annually to commemorate the descent of the Holy Spirit to the apostles 50 days after Easter |
| **carriage-cloth:** | upholstery |

| | |
|---|---|
| **skirls:** | shrill cries |
| **larking:** | playing about |
| **pomaded:** | treated with hair oil |
| **Odeon:** | branch of a cinema |
| **standing Pullmans:** | railway coaches waiting in a siding |

---

**'Faith Healing'** from *The Whitsun Weddings*

---

The scene is a meeting presided over by a visiting American faith-healer. The crowd is very large: the so-called healer has little time to spend on any individual. The effect, however, on the people in the audience is enormous and varied. Some leave; but some are unable to, because their experience with the faith healer – whether he has genuine gifts or not – has stirred up such depths in them. They find themselves projecting on to him all the thwarted wishes of their past lives; despite themselves they find themselves believing that he has a message for each individual.

In the third stanza the sense of this disturbance increases as Larkin suggests to us how many people suffer from not being loved enough; so fiercely do they feel this lack that they are willing to fill it with any experience, no matter how sham it might be. The last lines point up the ways in which, in everyday life, people keep themselves braced and defended against disappointment; what happens with the faith healer is that they are allowed to relax these defences, thawing into the long withheld tears; yet the final phrase, 'all time has disproved', ends the poem on a characteristically pessimistic tone, for if time has indeed disproved the possibility of real love, then what can a mere faith healer do about it?

COMMENTARY:
The crucial opposition in the poem is between the mechanical and suspect nature of the faith healer's ministrations and the stark reality of the emotions which get released in his presence. In the first stanza this is pointed up in the lines 'Within whose warm spring rain of loving care/Each dwells some twenty seconds'. The image of the spring rain also introduces us to the idea of people 'thawing', the ending, if only temporary, of a long icy winter which is Larkin's image for the way in which people are encouraged by the presence of the faith healer to relax their automatic defences.

In the second stanza the attitude of the narrator to the crowd becomes complicated. There is deep sympathy in the view of these people 'twitching and loud/With deep hoarse tears', people who are still waiting 'To re-awake at kindness'; but what do we feel when we read that 'Their thick tongues blort, their eyes squeeze grief'? Here we seem to be in the presence of people who are almost reduced to a debased, animal-like state. Behind this emotional complexity, we can sense a problem which Larkin is trying to explore: on the one hand there is a wish to be among these people, to be able to feel the moment of release, while on the other there is a conventional embarrassment at seeing people 'letting go' of themselves.

At the beginning of the third stanza it seems that a mood of scorn has taken over: 'Moustached in flowered frocks they shake'. But after that the poem grows increasingly lyrical as Larkin stands back from the scene and offers us a meditation on love and lovelessness. We are not asked to judge whether the feelings portrayed are accurate: that is whether these individuals really have been loved or not. What we are asked to recognise is that in all of us there survives a child who feels cheated of all the love that might have been his or hers; and it is this hidden child within who reawakes at the touch of the faith healer.

Is the faith healer genuine? We have no means of knowing. The persona seems to suggest he is not ('Their heads are clasped abruptly'); but then as the poem develops we see that the persona is himself not entirely to be trusted, he displays a certain envy of the situation. In the end it does not matter: as has been emphasised from the beginning, it is the voice of the faith healer which matters, the fact that he can say 'dear child' and *sound* sincere. Metaphorically, Larkin underlines that this is the depths ('deep American voice') speaking to the depths ('deep hoarse tears') and thus communicating at levels where our reason counts for nothing.

NOTES AND GLOSSARY:

**blort:**　　　　　Larkin's own word, to suggest 'blurting out', clumsiness, lack of control

---

**'Take One Home for the Kiddies'** from *The Whitsun Weddings*

---

On the surface, this is a poem about pets. Rabbits, hamsters, or whatever they are, we see them in the pet-shop window, far away from any kind of natural habitat and exposed to the stare of every passer-by. Naturally, children are attracted to them and persuade their mothers to buy them; but, as we see in the second stanza, the novelty soon wears off and the pets die.

COMMENTARY:

Under the surface, this is a highly complex poem, although this complexity is masked brilliantly by simplicity of language and syntax. Note, incidentally, a characteristically Larkin line in the first stanza,

'Huddled by empty bowls, they sleep', which is syntactically and rhythmically identical to a crucial line in 'Faith Healing', 'Moustached in flowered frocks they shake'.

Although we are sure it is pets that Larkin is talking about, he never says so directly, and in the first stanza this allows us to think more generally about others who may be 'Huddled by empty bowls', human victims of poverty and exploitation. The child's vision of this is direct but also thoughtlessly cruel: to the child these pets appear as mere possessions. There is a crucial ambiguity in the final word of the first stanza, 'keep': it has an ordinary, literal sense of owning a pet, but it also suggests the staving off of death. Either the pet itself will never die, or we somehow use pets as a reinforcement against our own deaths.

The second stanza is linguistically controlled by the extraordinary rhyming of 'novel' and 'shovel': the rapid, rather offhand sounds of these words, combined with the fact that to rhyme them at all suggests a certain sloppiness, both contribute to the offhand way in which Larkin is deliberately dealing with death in this stanza. There is nothing here of tragedy or grief, no real emotional intensity, no real perception of other creatures. There is not even a wish to explore the realities of death, and this is why Larkin uses the word 'somehow', to suggest the unexamined way in which people handle even matters of ultimate seriousness.

For the children, the death of their pet is just another game: '*Mam, we're playing funerals now*'. But if Larkin is likening these children to people at large, with their possessiveness and lack of thought and fellow-feeling, then the poem turns into a savage indictment of the limited level on which we all live; a poem about heartlessness and the absence of moral and emotional distinction.

Notice the careful patterning of sounds: the alliteration in the first line ('shallow' and 'shadeless') and in the third ('No dark, no dam') are designed to reinforce our sense of the inescapability of the pets' situation. But this alliteration returns with redoubled force towards the end ('Fetch the shoebox, fetch the shovel'), reminding us that what is really repetitive, really inevitable no matter what games we try to play with it, is death.

NOTES AND GLOSSARY:
**dam:** beavers make dams; but dam also means 'mother'

---

**'The Large Cool Store'** from *The Whitsun Weddings*

---

We are to picture a large shop selling clothing – quite a cheap shop, one where there is something for everybody to afford. The poet's eye strays over some of these clothes, and he thinks about the working people who are likely to wear them. But then his eye jumps to the 'Modes For Night', the stands of ladies' nightdresses. He sees these garments, their shapes and colours, and he senses a kind of misfit between the daylight world of factories and workaday clothes and this night-time world. Can these two worlds really be shared?

As he meditates on the problem, his mind turns over a number of solutions. It may be that at night we do move into a different world, that these 'Baby-Dolls and Shorties' are the nearest we can get to a contemporary representation of the 'differentness' of love. Or it may be that the difference is really one between men and women; that the sober 'browns and greys' belong to a world of men's work, whereas the 'Lemon, sapphire, moss-green, rose' are women's colours. Or it may be that these nightdresses represent only a fantasy about women; and if so that fantasy is not altogether a pleasant or coherent one since it requires women to be ever 'new', fresh and clean, and yet 'synthetic', since the materials he is describing are man-made (perhaps in both senses of the term). It requires of women that they represent ecstasy, passion, in an almost pornographic way, while at the same time being 'natureless', unnaturally clothed and unnatural in themselves.

COMMENTARY:

This is a difficult poem because it depends on a number of words which are quite specific to the time of its composition. Yet this very fact reminds us of one of the poem's themes, which is that these clothes are synthetic, throwaway, merely the stuff of a day's fashion.

At the beginning we sense no animosity on the poet's part: it is obviously good that there are cheap clothes available, that they are 'set out in simple sizes plainly' so that the purchaser can make sensible choices and see the goods on offer. Nevertheless, even here we wonder whether Larkin is also commenting on the poverty of lives led in 'low terraced houses', low in literal shape but also in the social order.

It is, however, when he observes the 'Modes For Night' that the tone becomes more critical. The word 'modes' is a pseudo-sophisticated word, meant to persuade us that these cheap clothes are like their high fashion equivalents, when we know really that they are 'machine-embroidered', cheaply made, mass produced.

They are thin and not made to last, so that we will always need to buy more. We also need to keep buying these clothes because they will rapidly go out of fashion; in this way they are designed to increase our consumption. The colours he uses are carefully chosen: 'lemon' is an obviously synthetic colour, as is 'rose'; 'sapphire' probably just means some garish shade of blue, but renamed to make it seem more attractive. 'Moss-green' reminds us sharply of the natural world, but only to contrast it with these 'unnatural' colours.

The materials ('Bri-Nylon') are also unnatural, as are the shapes, which are chosen artificially to exaggerate the female form. As they 'Flounce in clusters', they seem to have a life of their own.

We move, halfway through the third stanza, into a characteristic meditation on what these clothes mean about our relationships, our attitudes to each other. The 'they' of line 14 are the nightdresses; 'that world' is the other world, the grimy, darkened world of factories and terraced housing.

The three hypotheses Larkin offers us at the end are in descending order of pleasantness. He suggests to begin with that perhaps, even in a debased form, these clothes have to do with love, even with quite powerful emotions ('separate and unearthly'); for a moment, the poem flickers on the edge of romanticism. His next suggestion (which can be rearranged to read 'how separate and unearthly women are') is less acceptable, for it clearly relegates women to a different realm, as though there is an unbridgeable gap between the sexes. The third hypothesis, which is the one with which we are left, is less acceptable still since it suggests that these clothes embody only an infantile fantasy of women which does violence to their reality.

The poem is held together by a complex rhyme scheme. Each stanza rhymes ABABA, but the A lines in stanzas one and three also rhyme together (from 'clothes' down to 'shows'), as do the A lines in stanzas two and four, although in this case it is a half-rhyme (from 'houses' down to 'ecstasies'). The other tremendous skill Larkin shows here is of taking words from a common, throwaway vocabulary and using them to suggest an argument of depth and emotional strength.

NOTES AND GLOSSARY:

**Knitwear:** the term under which such a store would display jumpers, cardigans and the like

**Summer Casuals:** would include trousers and skirts of light material

**Hose:** socks, tights: like 'Modes', the word is a deliberately inflated one to persuade us of a spurious quality

**maroon:** brownish crimson

**navy:** navy blue

**Bri-Nylon:** a cheap, popular synthetic material, often used to make underwear

**Baby-Dolls and Shorties:** revealing nightwear for women

## 'Essential Beauty' from *The Whitsun Weddings*

The first stanza of this startling poem depends for its effect on the reader gradually realising that Larkin is talking about advertising hoardings. There are advertisements for bread, for custard, for motor-oil, for salmon; what they share is their complete inappropriateness to their surroundings ('screen graves with custard').

What the advertisements present is a composite view of how life should be: 'golden butter', 'Well-balanced families', 'fine/Midsummer weather'. These pictures of healthy outdoor life are balanced by an idealised picture of the home: 'cups at bedtime', 'slippers on warm mats'.

But at the break between the two stanzas Larkin states baldly that these pictures have little or nothing to do with the realities of life. They relate to the real only as 'pure crust, pure foam'; in the real world nothing can live up to these images of purity, and thus advertisements create and thrive on dissatisfaction and social envy. In the advertisements pubs are 'dark raftered' taverns where the elegant disport themselves; in reality drink causes distress and poverty, just as advertisements for cigarettes really cause people to die.

As they die, they have a vision: a vision of 'essential beauty'. They have thought that this beauty could be brought into their lives by obeying the injunctions on the hoardings; but in the end all we are shown is that this vision of beauty will always elude us in the very moment that we think we can reach out and grasp it.

COMMENTARY:

The very first line conjures up a vital image: these hoardings 'face all ways' not only in the literal sense but also in that they capture us at every point; there is no way we can escape their fantasised reflections of our desires. Thus the 'ends of streets' which are blocked are again not only literal but also the natural avenues of development which are 'blocked' by the lies which advertisements tell and the false tracks down which they send us.

The word 'groves' at the end of the fifth line is supposed to remind us of the sacred groves of ancient religions: advertising covers its objects with a sacred aura, but really there is nothing behind this apparent mystery – it is hollow and cruel.

The rhyming of 'gutter' and 'butter' is an apt summary of the principal contrast Larkin is drawing. These two worlds, he is saying, can be held together only if we believe in a kind of magic, the magic represented in the 'groves' and also in the gesture of the 'small cube', as if this cube, which is no doubt made of gravy powder, could somehow supply the key to another, better world.

Notice how the word 'aligned' in line 13 suggests how neatly ordered the world of advertising is, how it seems able to repel all disturbance and threat; in the advertisements even the cats are neatly 'quarter-profile' (and here, of course, Larkin is also using our own knowledge of the way in which cats actually do often seem to arrange themselves in the most prepossessing way!).

The opposition which Larkin draws at the end of the first and beginning of the second stanzas is summarised in the words 'reflect' and 'dominate'. These advertisements do not 'reflect', do not provide a recognisable image of the 'rained-on streets and squares'; rather, they display a world where the rain never falls, and thus provide images which seem more attractive than, and thus dominate, the outdoor world.

In the first part of the second stanza there are gentle hints that Larkin is mocking a Platonic view of the world. The Greek philosopher Plato claimed that the world which we see is purely insubstantial; to attain to wisdom and beauty we have to see through it to the 'essential' reality of things. Larkin is parodying this view in saying that the apparent reality of advertisements dissolves as we approach: their claim to represent a real vision is purely illusory.

The final image is one of the finest in Larkin. In it he manages to combine the everyday pathos of dying of lung cancer with a more universal image of the obscure object of desire. 'That unfocused she' is not a particular image; it is, as Larkin uses it, a summation of all the hopes and dreams which we have, those hopes and dreams which are exploited by advertising. The word 'recognising' in the last line has a multitude of implications: according to the syntactic structure, it is the 'unfocused she' who recognises the observer in the moment of his death, but clearly this meaning can also be reversed. The very fact that it can be reversed raises further doubts which move beyond the poem and which Larkin does nothing to allay: doubts about whether this object of desire really exists outside ourselves, or whether what we are really shown in advertising is a distorted image of our own self.

NOTES AND GLOSSARY:

| | |
|---|---|
| **cuts:** | choice pieces |
| **radiant bars:** | an image for (gas or electric) fires |
| **puking:** | vomiting |
| **pensioner:** | retired person |
| **halfpenny:** | half an old penny, approximately equivalent to one-sixth of a new penny |
| **smokers:** | meaning here cigarette smokers |
| **drag:** | slang for a pull on a cigarette |

## 'Toads Revisited' from *The Whitsun Weddings*

This poem, of course, develops from the poem called 'Toads', and in one sense is a reply to the argument raised there about why it is necessary to work.

Here the persona spends most of the poem toying with the idea of not working, and how it would feel. But the images he comes up with are curiously, and deliberately, empty. 'Walking around in the park' may sound pleasant in a limited way, but it is also purposeless, repetitive, without shape or design; and this is the main problem the persona encounters, how to give shape to a life which is without work. 'Not a bad place to be' is rather weak advocacy; and indeed the people he encounters in the park are all weak, all people who obviously have proved unable to take the strain of life – very different, we notice, from the more envied outcasts of 'Toads'.

What all these 'characters' have in common, says Larkin, is that they are 'all dodging the toad work', they are all 'stupid or weak'. But here again we encounter the problem we came across with 'Toads', which is about the level of irony in the poem. Are we meant to agree with the persona in his rather cursory assessment of the people in the park? Or are we meant to think that he is rationalising, preparing for himself suspect arguments about why it is better to go on working by claiming to despise those who do not?

These people, he claims, are all passive: they watch the bread being delivered, they hear the clocks, they see those, like the children, who have places to be at fixed times. But they themselves can do nothing but reflect aimlessly on their 'failures'; they have no community to which to belong.

Faced with these images, the persona not surprisingly opts to return to the world of work (maybe simply to return to the office after a meditative lunch hour) and to settle back into a routine which, at least, gives one a sense of purpose in life. The force of the last image is to suggest that, when all comes down to dust, we all need some kind of comfort, a prop with which to get through the days; work is just such a prop, and therefore although we know that in one sense it will prove to be deadly, nevertheless it can help us on the unavoidable journey.

COMMENTARY:

There is something determinedly casual about much of this poem, especially near the beginning where even the rhymes seem throwaway and lines like 'the grass to lie on' barely seem to say anything at all. Part of the point of this is to suggest that the persona's vision is itself 'blurred', like the background noises: he is not yet really focusing on the world of the park, and perhaps this is because he does not want to; he has no wish to face what the reality of not working would be like.

But during the third stanza the scene comes starkly alive with the 'palsied old step-takers' and 'hare-eyed clerks', as though the persona can no longer avoid the terror of these shapeless lives as they intrude upon him.

The sense he is trying to conjure up here is like that which many of us have felt when excused school through illness, yet able to move about. There is a pleasure at being released from everyday life but also a doubt, amounting in the case of the 'hare-eyed' clerks to an image of panic, about what to do with the time. And beyond this lies an image of sickness, the 'waxed-fleshed out-patients'; the proximity of this image to that of the people in long coats, the tramps looking for what they can find in rubbish bins, may also remind us of the people in long coats who come running across the fields in 'Days' and remind us of the inevitability of sickness and death.

'The sun by clouds covered' is a curious line; it appears too 'poetic', too deliberately artificial to belong in such a colloquial poem. Perhaps Larkin inserts it here to suggest reverie and meditation: to say that, yes, given this freedom it would be possible to drift away (like the clouds), but would we be able to stand that drifting away, the lack of conventional supports and comforts?

His irony returns in the rhyming of 'failures' and 'lobelias', which has the effect of reducing what might be the failure of an entire life to triviality. In the last two stanzas that irony is clearly also directed at himself: it is as though the persona sees how repetitive his own life – as a librarian? – is, but sees also that he has no choice. Paradoxically, although he has accused the characters 'outside' of being weak we are allowed to entertain the possibility that it is the protagonist who is himself weak, unable to take the risk of moving away from his desk, his routine.

But if that is so, says Larkin, then it is a weakness we all share, for it is the common weakness of being unable to face death, and the toad work, whatever its deficiencies, at least helps to mark our days and to prevent us from a slow meaningless drift towards obliteration: 'by clouds covered'.

NOTES AND GLOSSARY:

**palsied:** trembling

**step-takers:** people who are able to walk only extremely slowly, one step at a time

**hare-eyed:** looking permanently scared

**jitters:** physical shakes; also fears

| | |
|---|---|
| **out-patients:** | hospital patients who are not ill enough to be admitted residentially; also playing on the notion of the outdoors |
| **lobelias:** | blue-flowered plants common in gardens |
| **loaf-haired:** | referring to a peculiarly unattractive way of arranging the hair |

---

## 'Dockery and Son' from *The Whitsun Weddings*

In this poem the protagonist returns to his old college, and finds himself involved in a conversation about a person called Dockery who was at college at the same time. He is told that Dockery's son is now a student there.

He meditates on the time he spent at the college, remembering past incidents in a generalised way, and eventually catches a train and leaves. On the train he tries to remember Dockery and fails. But what catches his imagination is the thought that, for the dates to be right, Dockery, whoever he was, must have had a son when only nineteen or twenty.

The protagonist does not get much further in his reverie for the moment, for he falls asleep, waking up when he has to change trains at Sheffield. At the station he walks to the end of the platform and looks out over the railway lines, seeing them as an image of how lives come together and diverge again. He is thinking partly of the mysterious Dockery and himself, but also, as Larkin then tells us, of his own aloneness, an aloneness to which he had thought himself reconciled but which now suddenly appears in a different light when he contrasts himself with his own fantasy of Dockery and what he must have been like.

Yet the fourth and fifth stanzas, although they show us the protagonist wrestling with these problems, come to no direct conclusion. Instead he is sidetracked into wondering about habit in general, how it is that he is in his position – 'no son, no wife/No house or land' – while other people are in quite different positions. It has, he thinks, very little to do with our conscious ambitions and desires; rather, habit is something which happens to you, inexorably, throughout life, and it is only when it is too late that you realise how closely it has bound you into its web.

This sense of a weight – the 'sand-clouds' which bear us towards death – and the protagonist's reawakened sense of being alone combine in a powerful final quatrain which tells us that nothing can really reconcile us to the passing of time and the loss of hope. No matter therefore how we live our lives, all difference is reduced to sameness by the imminence of death, 'the only end of age'.

COMMENTARY:
This poem is a particularly fine example of the way in which Larkin manages to work ordinary rhythms of speech and thought into a subtle poetic structure. Consider, for example, the direct speech of the first stanza, or the sleepy reverie of the third.

The heart of the poem is, appropriately, to be found in the image at its centre, that of the joining and parting lines. The 'strong/ Unhindered moon' relates oddly to this image; after all, the way in which the moon is actually reflected in railway lines is in fragments, and perhaps this irony is intended. At any rate the moon here stands for a kind of isolation which, in a certain light, may look proud and strong but in another can come to seem merely defensive.

Certainly the central character is himself defensive: his attempts to explain Dockery seem simultaneously to suggest how inapplicable all this is to himself, as if indeed he is trying to protect himself with numbness from the 'shock' of this sudden realisation of a descent into lonely old age. But there is, of course, no possibility of going back; we know this from the beginning when the protagonist tries to return to his old college room. The fact that the door is 'locked' is given heavy emphasis by the position of the word, and the image of the locked door into the past recurs in the fifth stanza.

The structure towards the end becomes complicated as the protagonist's own thoughts, which have been wandering, become inexorably focused on the issues raised by Dockery; or rather, by his associations with Dockery, since it is one of the points of the poem that the identity of Dockery remains in doubt throughout. 'Not from what/We think truest, or most want to do' refers to the failure of our beliefs and desires; we may think we want certain things, but we are overtaken by 'habit', by a fixed style, although we can never see how this carapace was first formed.

The 'sand-clouds' are thick, choking, deathly, but they are each formed in our own image, our doom is in each case appropriate to something we cannot perceive in ourselves. The couplet 'Life is first boredom, then fear./Whether or not we use it, it goes' has a curiously jaunty rhythm, as though the protagonist is trying to revert to the carelessness he had known earlier; but this last attempt at a defence against death fails at the end as we are made to realise the fallibility and impotence of our reason and our will.

NOTES AND GLOSSARY:
**Dean:** college official
**death-suited:** 1) black-suited, formally dressed; 2) dressed as for a funeral – Dockery's? His own? 3) 'apt' for death

| | |
|---|---|
| **half-tight:** | half-drunk |
| **who was killed:** | in the Second World War, we may presume |
| **Sheffield:** | a Northern town being used here as an image of industry as opposed to the peace of the college |
| **warp:** | become stuck, usually through damp |
| **patronage:** | Larkin is here suggesting that, just as for some people a growing son reminds them of their own age, so for him this growing sense of 'nothing' occupies a parallel role – or a worse one? |

---

## 'High Windows' from *High Windows*

---

At first reading this is one of the most baffling of Larkin's poems, because it concludes with an image – the image, furthermore, which he used again as the title of a collected volume – which, although beautiful and resonant in itself, appears to have very little connection with the main body of the poem.

The protagonist is an ageing man reflecting on the generation gap. He sees two young people and guesses that they make love, something which would have been unthinkable when he was their age. He says he knows that this freedom is desirable ('paradise'); but when he adds that the young are 'going down the long slide/To happiness, endlessly', one wonders whether he is not projecting some of his own feelings into the youngsters.

He seems to take a rueful pleasure in being part of a generation which is being 'pushed to one side', and then thinks back to his own youth and wonders whether the older generation then looked upon his generation with this half-ironic envy. And it is this thought which seems to lead him into the final image, the image of 'high windows'.

COMMENTARY:
We immediately notice the contrast in the poem between at least two registers of language. The vocabulary of the first stanza and of parts of the fourth is crude, even violent: this in part reflects the protagonist's own feelings, although perhaps he is disguising this by pretending inside himself that this is the kind of language which the young themselves use.

The last stanza, however, seems entirely different, confronting us with the problem of what these 'high windows' are. They conjoin an image of freedom – the 'deep blue air' – with a sense of exclusion from it; the reader is reminded of a nineteenth-century schoolroom, where the windows would be placed high off the ground so that no distractions from the outside world were felt. There is also a subsidiary connotation of church windows, 'high' in the other sense.

What connects the poem together, then, is Larkin's sense that although he is in the presence of something called freedom, he is never able to share in it except vicariously; perhaps this is the plight of the poet.

Notice also the image of the outdated combine harvester, the piece of farm machinery left to rust in the fields. The passage in italics, representing the voice of a past older generation, speaks of religious fears and conventions which have now been brushed aside, left to rot; although this appears to refer to a time 'forty years back', perhaps it also refers to a voice which is still present in Larkin's mind, the voice of guilt which is the inverse side, as it were, of free love.

The 'long slide' suggests an absence of restraint; these young people have freed themselves of parental and religious constraints, and yet perhaps the idea that they have done so successfully is itself a fantasy.

This brings us back to the last stanza; for although we may interpret this as an exclusion from freedom, the image itself remains one of astonishing beauty, and perhaps at the end of the day there is a hint of a different, further meaning which is that complete freedom is unreal. Perhaps it is better to experience freedom in this bounded way, through the 'high windows'; perhaps the 'framing' of freedom within conventions might in the end be more satisfying than a total freedom which may end up, as in the vocabulary of the first stanza, by valuing nothing and providing no shape to the 'long slide'.

NOTES AND GLOSSARY:

**kids:** slang for children, young people

**fucking:** slang for making love

**pills:** contraceptive pills

**diaphragm:** a female contraceptive device

**bloody:** a swearword, here intended to convey the envy of the speaker

**sun-comprehending:** Larkin appears to mean that the glass 'comprehends' the sun in the sense of understanding it, but also 'includes' or frames it

---

## 'Annus Mirabilis' from *High Windows*

---

This poem, like 'High Windows', is a reflection on the generation gap and on the sudden changes in the behaviour of young people which occurred during the 1960s, although it seems at first sight to take a more jaunty, careless approach to the subject, as evidenced in the 'choric' repetitions of the first and last stanzas and in the rhythm structure throughout.

The persona flippantly points out in the first stanza that although life has changed for many people as a result of the breaking down of social *mores*, he is rather too old for these changes to affect him and is thus left out. In the second stanza he contrasts the contemporary notions of free love with the situation between the sexes in the past, in his own youth, where everything sexual was coloured by 'shame' and was thus reduced to 'A sort of bargaining' in which each potential partner tried to get what they wanted by underhand means.

On the face of it he is glad this time has passed and that the 'quarrel', the difference between the wishes of boys and girls, men and women, has been resolved; but in the third stanza his images become so strong – 'A quite unlosable game' – that one cannot avoid feeling that there is irony here and that therefore the tone of 'life was never better' (itself a version of the famous slogan 'You never had it so good', coined in the 1960s by Prime Minister Harold Macmillan) is not merely celebratory but also a kind of warning to the young, and to society at large, that this kind of self-satisfied pleasure might well be only a prelude to something much worse.

COMMENTARY:
To say that 'Sexual intercourse began/In nineteen sixty-three' is obviously ironic; what Larkin means is, first, that it became possible to speak publicly about sex at that time, and second, that young people of the time have the *illusion* that, because of this, they are the inventors of sexual pleasure. The lifting of the ban on D. H. Lawrence's novel, *Lady Chatterley's Lover*, was a milestone in the relaxation in censorship. The pop group The Beatles were widely regarded as the first incarnation of the new, freer spirit of the 1960s.

The second stanza gives a sour picture of the past, looking back to the post-war years of austerity in economic and moral terms. The contrast between this and the succeeding stanza is crucial. The past is made to represent a 'wrangle', a struggle for scarce economic and emotional resources within the constraints of a non-expanding world, whereas the present is seen as a time when restraints have been lifted, when everybody can be a winner. Obviously, although perhaps it took a poet to realise what economists and politicians of the time refused to realise, a condition in which everybody wins is an illusion, and Larkin means us to notice this and to recognise in the imagery of 'A brilliant breaking of the bank,/A quite unlosable game' the self-delusion of the gambler, an inability to realise that such a condition is bound to be a purely temporary one.

So the final stanza is open to two different interpretations. On one level the protagonist seems quite content to rest within this illusion, rueful though his sense of his own age may be; on a deeper level, he is calling the reader's attention to the short-sightedness of this view and inviting us to criticise it.

The rhythms of the poem are intended to suggest the lyrics of a pop song, with its emphasis on instant pleasure; thus the popular tone of the poem is in ironic contrast to its Latin title, meaning 'Year of Wonders'.

NOTES AND GLOSSARY:

**LP:**           long-playing record (itself a new medium in the 1960s)

---

## 'The Explosion' from *High Windows*

This is a poem about an explosion in a coalmine, and more specifically about a rumour that at the moment of the explosion, in which many miners died, their wives at home knew it was happening and saw visions of their husbands. The rhythms are unusual for Larkin, conjuring up a kind of solemn processional, emphasised in particular by the Church text which constitutes the sixth stanza.

Larkin begins by imagining a state of quiet which is nonetheless ominous ('Shadows pointed towards the pithead'). He presents to us the miners; they are rough, loud, but vital; although they work underground, they still have some contact with the world of nature, shown by the reference to rabbits and larks' eggs, and they retain a gentleness, evidenced in the lodging of the eggs in the grasses.

Their passing through the gates is literally their entry into the works of the mine, but symbolically we are also reminded of an entry into death's kingdom. The only outward sign of the explosion deep underground is a 'tremor', and the deaths are only registered by the cows who stop chewing 'for a second'. But this movement is reflected at a different level by the entry into the poem of a solemn moment from a funeral service.

This text, however, is not merely inserted by the poet; it is also said to have been part of the set of visions seen by the womenfolk. They saw the text, and they saw their husbands, already dead, walking towards them, larger than life. Larkin makes no attempt to explain this extraordinary phenomenon.

COMMENTARY:

This poem is very rare among Larkin's works in being entirely free from irony. It is a solemn, sad poem which recounts to us a mystery and is content to leave any explanation of that mystery to us.

This imagery is closely worked: notice, for example, how the closeness of an entire community, soon to be shattered by death, is indicated in a single line, 'Fathers, brothers, nicknames, laughter', which shades from the factual into a lightly-sketched account of how the men relate to each other, suggesting that they have all been related since birth, that they know each other beyond words.

The 'shadows' and the sleeping 'slagheap' of the first stanza are tied by alliteration to the 'sun' of stanza five, 'scarfed' as in a heat-haze; what is conjured up here is a sense of sleeping which is disturbed only lightly by the tremendous and violent events below the ground, which in turn emphasises the strangeness and inexplicability of the women's visions.

We see much of the imagery drawn together in the last full stanza and the floating last line. In death these men are 'larger than life', creating a contrast with the belittling effect of life as a miner, and this sense is further emphasised by the phrase 'they managed', as though even when alive these men only just managed to live, financially as well as in terms of the everyday risks which miners run.

'Gold as on a coin' indicates the way in which these men – during life blackened and debased, 'Coughing oath-edged talk and pipe-smoke' – can only be transformed by death into something of value; perhaps it is only through the shock of something like this explosion that mine-owners can be brought to realise the human value of their workers. The word 'somehow' emphasises the way in which the women themselves were not concerned, or able, to make sense of their visions, thus contributing to a suggestion that they were real and not, for example, imagined for the sake of gain. The unbroken eggs are a powerful image of gentleness, care, a summary of all the virtues of community, marriage, life together which have been shattered by this explosion and by those responsible for it.

NOTES AND GLOSSARY:

**moleskins:** thick trousers worn in the countryside

**nicknames:** slang names used between close friends or relatives

**scarfed:** wrapped; here also, perhaps, protected from the violence below

---

**'The Card-Players'** from *High Windows*

---

Like 'The Explosion' this is an unusual poem for Larkin, although for quite different reasons. It is an attempt to call to mind, or reconstruct, a painting from a very particular period, a seventeenth-century Dutch painting, and the way in which Larkin portrays his characters is designed to correspond very closely to the heavy, clumping, rural tones of this kind of art.

The names of the characters are invented so as to combine typical Dutch spelling with meanings which are obscene in English (see Glossary). The observer of the poem sees this scene, a scene of drunkenness, gambling and swearing, but he has a double reaction. Perhaps this is well summarised in the image of Old Prijck's 'skull face' being 'firelit': the face like a skull belongs to the world of death, cold, the dark, whereas the firelight which illuminates this imagined interior belongs to the world of life, warmth, colour. The protagonist seems to see the scene as loathsome in its animality, but yet to be envied for the unquestioning communal warmth which it possesses.

This doubleness of mind is well conjured in the final, 'The secret, bestial peace!', where the protagonist seems to be admiring, envying and despising all at the same time. All of these emotions are, obviously, directed at the kind of bucolic scene he is depicting and which can be found in Dutch painting, but they are also, perhaps, directed at painting and thus art itself in a general way, which is 'secret' and 'bestial' in the ways in which it moves people without their knowledge or acquiescence.

COMMENTARY:

The principal conflict in this poem is between opposing attitudes on the part of the persona himself. His contempt is clearly shown in the opening: 'Jan van Hogspeuw staggers to the door/And pisses at the dark'. This is a world of animal impulse, bestial drunkenness, mindless sinking into degraded behaviour. Even the identities of the people are not secure: 'someone behind drinks ale', as though there are many other Jans and Dirks, all undifferentiated.

But there is more here than contempt, and this hinges particularly on the symbol of the cards. At the surface level these are simply playing cards on which to gamble, but we sense below this a relationship between the cards and the stereotyped characters in the painting, so that we are reminded of the Tarot pack.

Notice that as soon as 'Dirk deals the cards' we are moved, as if by magic, out from the hot interior to the 'surrounding starlessness', as though there is something in the cards which reminds us of a greater and more frightening world far away from the comforts of home. The word 'starlessness' perhaps also serves to remind us of the direction-lessness of man: how he would 'follow the star' if he could, even by practising astrology, but in this condition of 'starlessness' there are only the cards to turn to.

But perhaps we do not want to wander out into this dubious, dark world; perhaps we would sooner stay in our cave, which represents home, in which we can be shielded, if only for a time, from the terrifying knowledge of the outside. And perhaps, therefore, this is what painting is for, to shield us from a journey outside. That outside may be populated by the eternal forms represented by 'Rain, wind and fire', but in here, in the world of home and maybe also in the world of vicarious, aesthetic pleasure, there is instead 'The secret, bestial peace' which proffers its own values and suffers us its own enjoyments.

NOTES AND GLOSSARY:

| | |
|---|---|
| **Hogspeuw:** | pun on 'hog', a male pig, and 'spew', meaning to vomit |
| **pisses:** | slang for urinates |
| **Dogstoerd:** | pun on 'dog' and 'turd', meaning excrement |
| **clay:** | meaning a clay pipe |
| **Prijck:** | pun on 'prick', slang word for penis |
| **ham-hung:** | with hams hanging from them |
| **farts:** | slang for passing wind |
| **gobs:** | slang for spits |

## 'This Be The Verse' from *High Windows*

This strange poem has become one of Larkin's most famous; perhaps its brevity and simplicity make it peculiarly memorable.

Bringing together themes from, for example, 'Dockery and Son' and 'High Windows', Larkin here explores the question of what the generations pass on to one another yet again, but there is an unrelieved bleakness to this poem which sets it apart from many earlier ones. The tone is set at the beginning, 'They fuck you up, your mum and dad', and intensifies in the second stanza where, first, we are told that this pain in the transition between the generations is nothing new but the inescapable stuff of history, and second, we are treated to the voice of casualness, the tones of a poetic persona for whom the past holds nothing but a prefiguration of the awfulness of the present.

The third stanza seems to start with a grand generalisation, 'Man hands on misery to man', and the solemnity of this is increased by the smoothly beautiful rhythms of 'It deepens like a coastal shelf'; but this 'poeticisation' is deliberately wrecked by the crudity and violence of the last two lines.

COMMENTARY:
What are we really meant to make of poems like this, which sound unrelievedly pessimistic? Certainly they cannot be 'saved' from this pessimism, but we can look more closely at Larkin's stance here, for instance by noting the relation between the poem and its title.

The title suggests religion, a lesson read out at Sunday-morning service, whereas the poem itself exists in an inexorably secular world. This tension is part of the point: just as the world of religion constitutes a critique of everyday reality, so the ordinary world mocks religious pretensions. What is important is the 'misfit' between religion, ideals, codes of moral behaviour, value systems, on the one hand, and on the other, the casual valuelessness implicit in this poem and also, as Larkin sees it, in most of the secularised world around him.

What this moves towards is a real nihilism whereby the only answer to the great questions of life comes in the form of the petty, crude aphorism, 'Get out as early as you can,/And don't have any kids yourself'. It is not so much the advice which is shocking but the *tone* of the advice, which makes it sound as though life is not only not worth living, it is not even worthy of serious, thoughtful comment.

NOTES AND GLOSSARY:

**fuck you up:** here principally means 'mess you up'

**soppy-stern:** Larkin's own compound, including strictness *and* sentimentality

**coastal shelf:** the shallow waters around a coastline, which suddenly give way to the ocean depths a certain distance out

---

**'Going, Going'** from *High Windows*

This is a meditative poem, although with Larkin the term 'meditation' often seems too strong for what *looks* like a stream of random reflections.

The subject is the disappearance of Britain's countryside. The poet begins by saying that, on the whole, he has always thought that the countryside, and some kind of balance between the rural and the urban, would survive for his lifetime. He has known that traditional ways of life are under threat, but he has assumed that these threats were for the most part 'false alarms'; and even if the sprawl of the suburbs does increase, he has assumed – selfishly – that he and people like him will still be able to find the countryside by driving out to it.

In the third stanza he moves to a generalisation, that 'nature' is stronger, more resilient than man; that however we may damage it with pollution and other forms of carelessness, it will always somehow be able to clean itself and recover.

At the end of this stanza, however, he registers a change of feeling, although he is unable to say clearly why that change has occurred.

Does he increasingly doubt the ability of nature to survive the onslaughts on it, or is it simply that he is growing older? At any event he sees the rising generation as marked by an increasing greed and by an increasing emphasis on profit at the expense of care for the environment – the 'ten/Per cent more in the estuaries' is more pollution, more refuse, more sludge.

To the poet this appears as a speeding up of the process whereby everything will end up 'bricked in', except for parts of the country preserved for the sake of tourism. All that will remain of England will be memories and those bits and pieces which will survive in museums; for the people, there will be a world composed of 'concrete and tyres'.

In the last stanza he gloomily points out that probably nobody really intends this to happen, but then, intention is not necessary; already things have drifted a very long way, and he thinks that there is nothing to prevent them from drifting farther still.

COMMENTARY:
The title refers to the language of the auctioneer who, when selling something to the highest bidder, will say 'Going – going – gone' before the hammer comes down. This suggests the image of parts of the country being sold off to those who can pay most, with no regard for the social cost.

The rhythm is fast, apparently casual, reflecting the carelessness which the poet sees all around him. Some of the stanzas flow into each other without due regard for the endings of lines and this is deliberate, reflecting his sense of an unstoppable drift or flow away from a more orderly, responsible society towards one where nothing is planned and no account is taken of people's real needs – as opposed to those false needs which he mentions in the last stanza, which are simply justifications for our greed.

He feels rueful about the passing away of an older order: in the first stanza he clearly does not admire the 'louts', yet they represent a more communal world where everybody had their place, and are thus perhaps preferable to the screaming kids of the fourth stanza.

The 'bleak high-risers' of the second stanza are blocks of flats, but also the people who live in them, whose outlook is bleak.

At the beginning of the third stanza he uses the word 'just' in two ways: in terms of obvious clause structure it connects with the second line, but the first line including 'just' is also an entity in its own right, suggesting the precarious balance between nature and man and how easily that balance may be overturned.

Throughout the poem Larkin refuses to attribute simple blame for this condition. 'The crowd . . . in the M1 café' may offend him in many ways, but their taste, or lack of it, is not their own fault. We get nearer to the heart of the cause of the imminent catastrophe in the fifth stanza, where the 'spectacled grins' represent the blandness of businessmen as they contemplate a commercial manoeuvre without taking account of the possible human consequences. What is important here though is the fact that these are indeed mere 'grins', not whole people.

The phrase 'Grey area grants' is bitter with irony. What Larkin is saying is that successive governments have failed to maintain 'green areas', places where industry and commerce should not be allowed to interfere with the environment; all we can do now is to allow industry yet more expansion and thus convert the green into grey – and worse, help industry to move there because it will save them expense.

Larkin determinedly refuses to convert his observations into a political analysis. In the sixth stanza he takes up the position of the ordinary observer. He does not bother to complete the sentence about getting to the sea because he assumes everybody will know to what he is referring: the traffic jams, the pollution, the commercialisation. And he follows this up by insisting that this is just his personal impression – 'It seems, just now'.

The last line of the seventh stanza is hard to make out: does Larkin really mean that England is in the hands of 'crooks and tarts', or does he mean that this is the *impression* England now gives? Perhaps he means to leave the question open.

'The shadows, the meadows, the lanes' summarise the countryside but are perhaps also a reference to the great artist of rural England, John Constable.

In the last stanza he equates motivation – 'greeds' – and their effects – 'garbage' – to intensify his argument, but returns again to insist that this is just his individual, amateurish perception – 'I just think it will happen, soon.' The strength of this formulation is that he means to remind us that, really, he is not alone in this feeling: that many of us, with similar unsystematic impotence, share it.

NOTES AND GLOSSARY:

**louts:** unruly youths
**split-level shopping:** shopping malls
**M1:** the first motorway in Britain
**Business Page:** in a newspaper
**estuaries:** areas of water at the mouths of rivers
**snuff it:** colloquial (and casual) for 'dying'
**the whole/Boiling:** a slang expression for the whole thing
**crooks and tarts:** criminals and prostitutes; but the half-jocular

|            |                                                      |
|------------|------------------------------------------------------|
|            | terms suggest to us that their criminality is not to be taken too seriously |
| **guildhalls:** | here, medieval civic buildings                   |
| **carved:** | notice that, in accordance with the rhythm, this should be read here as a two-syllable word; itself a relevant archaism |
| **choirs:** | here, short for choir-stalls                         |
| **galleries:** | art galleries, museums                            |

---

## 'The Building' from *High Windows*

---

Like 'Essential Beauty', this poem depends initially on tension between the description and the location; we are in a hospital, but Larkin lets the fact grow on us gradually.

Initially the building is presented as a thing of beauty, a 'lucent comb' which is (notice the alliteration) 'Higher than the handsomest hotel'. At the end we are offered another image, the 'clean-sliced cliff', which suggests the correlation between the building and the precipice of death; what, we are therefore asked, is all this 'building' for when our own lives might collapse in a moment?

In the first stanza we are invited to contrast the apparent modernity of the hospital with the surrounding streets 'out of the last century', and throughout the poem we can reflect on a contrast between efficiency and scruffiness. The language used shows Larkin at his most brilliant, impersonating the everyday reader with colloquial and imprecise phrases like 'tea at so much a cup', 'ripped mags'.

He impersonates also the person attending hospital who does not properly understand what is going on – which is, after all, our usual condition in a hospital, whether we are recognisably ill or not. Thus at the end of the second stanza 'a kind of nurse' arrives; she picks out somebody from the waiting-room, apparently at random, just as death will take us at random and without explanation.

In the fourth stanza this innocence about the purposes of hospitals increases as we are invited to suppose that the grandeur of the hospital, its obvious costliness, reflects how seriously we may have 'gone wrong', as though we were machines which can only be understood or, we hope, repaired by a skilled mechanic.

Larkin picks out, as in the 'Toads' poems, the sense of how odd it is, on a working day, to be in an unusual place, and yet how suspiciously we view those similarly picked out ('how their eyes/Go to each other, guessing'). He also emphasises throughout the peculiar solemnity of being in hospital: 'They're quiet', partly out of individual fear, partly from a realisation that this condition of being sick is something which all of us will come to in the end.

The outside world seems approachable, yet in hospital we are held away from it, and it is remarkable, Larkin says, how quickly the world of the ordinary, where 'girls with hair-dos fetch/Their separates from the cleaners', becomes a foreign place while we take up our place in the ranks of the sick, the malfunctioning.

Being in hospital obliterates all distinction of age, of gender: 'All know they are going to die'. It is not, of course, that everybody is going to die in *this* hospital, but that being in hospital reminds us, if only temporarily, of the inescapability of death. And yet, Larkin suggests at the end, the hospital also reminds us of all the effort put into the 'struggle to transcend', the effort to postpone at least, although nothing can possibly do this, least of all the act represented in the final, floating line, of visiting the sick with 'wasteful, weak, propitiatory flowers'.

COMMENTARY:
The flowers at the end are 'propitiatory' because they are intended, unconsciously, to stave off, to postpone the operations of physical sickness, to 'propitiate' the gods. There is a sense throughout the poem that the modern concept of medicine is only a small part of the purpose of hospitals; that the deeper purpose is to erect some kind of 'building', some symbol of the solid and even the soaring in the face of the inevitability of physical decline. The hospital becomes almost a magical place, although it is doubtful whether this magic is effective.

The first stanza portrays the faulty body as a breathing chest, sighing in its uncertainty. This superhuman image is immediately contrasted with the 'scruffy' porters and the ambulances, the frightening smell, all too physical reminders of the physical reality of the hospital. The key contrast throughout is between the everyday normalcy of 'paperbacks, and tea at so much a cup' and death; Larkin emphasises the state of terrified docility into which we are put by our encounters with sickness, our own or others': we are 'those who tamely sit'.

The word 'humans' erupts into the third stanza unexpectedly, reminding us of what we all have in common even though we may not want to be reminded of it; for what we have in common is mortality, which constitutes a 'ground curiously neutral'.

The notion of 'confession' in the fourth stanza is important, suggesting as it does that the hospital, even medicine as a whole practice, may now occupy a place in people's lives similar to the place occupied by the Church in past ages, a point emphasised and refined by the image of the 'cathedral' towards the end. It is as though the hospital has become the best we can do in terms of offering something to the powers of life and death.

The phrase 'how tall/It's grown by now' has at least three meanings: it refers to the hospital, to our anxiety at being there, and to the disease which may be growing inside us.

The phrase 'as they climb/To their appointed levels' again invokes the ironic comparison between the hospital and religion: this is indeed a heaven or a hell in which we find ourselves, especially in the sense that there is nothing we can do as individuals to avoid our fate. The notion of 'rooms past those' and so on intensifies this image by reminding us of Dante's circle of hell, from which there is no escape.

A contrast, then, is being pointed here between the mundanity of illness and the sacred aura with which death might be surrounded, beneficially or otherwise, in other cultures: this is further emphasised by the apostrophe 'O world,/Your loves, your chances' which suggests how inappropriate any sort of romanticising might be to the facts of sickness, especially when considered on a mass scale.

The 'unseen congregations' return us to the problematic relation between the hospital and the church: clearly in the hospital the coming of death is celebrated as a sort of ritual, but is it the right sort? Or are we reduced by modern mass medicine to a condition of passivity in which we cannot understand even our own passing?

NOTES AND GLOSSARY:

| | |
|---|---|
| **lucent:** | shining, bright |
| **comb:** | Larkin means to compare the many-windowed hospital to a honeycomb |
| **mags:** | short for magazines |
| **lagged:** | covered, probably rather shabbily, to prevent loss of heat |
| **kids chalk games:** | the reference is probably to hopscotch, a jumping game which involves chalk marks on the pavement |
| **hair-dos:** | the implication is of cheap, standardised ways of arranging the hair |
| **separates:** | Larkin is using the jargon of sellers and cleaners of clothes to refer to skirts, blouses, etc. (note the term picked up in 'separately' five lines further on) |
| **four:** | four o'clock |

# Part 3

# Commentary

## Themes

Larkin's poems are very often about himself. If we think of 'The Whitsun Weddings', 'High Windows' or the 'Toads' poems, we see thoughts and reflections very close to the surface which impress us as Larkin's own. There is much use of the first-person pronoun ('That Whitsun, I was late getting away', 'At first, I didn't notice what a noise/The weddings made', 'Struck, I leant/More promptly out next time'); there are references, such as the ones to the 'in-tray' and the 'loaf-haired secretary' in 'Toads Revisited', which seem very close to Larkin's life as a librarian.

But the self which Larkin presents to us is a curious one and, like all such poetic personae, carefully constructed. It is not the intricate, clever, articulate self of much metaphysical poetry, nor is it the wildly emotional self of romanticism; rather, Larkin's is a self which is very much at the mercy of outside forces. Many of his poems – 'Dockery and Son' is a good example – seem to be attempts to realise something, but with very great difficulty: we do not receive only the conclusions but the whole process of reflection, and this reflection can be a very jumpy, occasional process. Larkin's progression in 'Dockery and Son' from his encounter at his old college to his final general observations on age and death is not a linear one, but is compounded of the seemingly random experiences of his train journey – the 'awful pie', the 'Joining and parting lines'.

What Larkin seems to be saying is that the self is only very rarely capable of coherent, continuous thoughts. For most of the time we are pushed this way and that by our encounters with the outside world; we are all at the mercy of forces greater than ourselves, and to pretend otherwise is merely to deal in ideals and abstractions. In this way, although Larkin appears to be talking about himself, he is seeing himself very much as typical of everyman: life proceeds in jerks, fits and starts, like a stopping train, and his best poems try to recount that experience which is compounded of pressures, accidents, habits, all of which are stronger than our will.

This links naturally to his second theme, which is the enormous pressure of contemporary life. Everywhere we are surrounded by messages telling us to do things or not to do things: 'Essential Beauty' is a particularly vivid example of this, with its huge advertising hoardings which

> block the ends of streets with giant loaves,
> Screen graves with custard, cover slums with praise
> Of motor-oil and cuts of salmon . . .

These advertisements represent a world of false values or, better, a world in which there are no values at all because everything is reduced to identical images. In this world we lose our power of discrimination, and human life itself becomes worthless.

In 'Going, Going' he puts this sense of creeping dehumanisation very clearly when he says that

> For the first time I feel somehow
> That it isn't going to last,

> That before I snuff it, the whole
> Boiling will be bricked in
> Except for the tourist parts –
> First slum of Europe . . .

Notice again in the first of these lines the word 'somehow': Larkin is not trying to persuade us that he has a worked-out political position or even that he can justify his sense of despair in rational terms. Rather, he is speaking of the doubtful and bewildered feelings which are occasionally common to all of us when we suspect that things in the world around us have got out of control. It is not so much that we are being manipulated; more that nobody retains any sense of the whole of British society, and thus there are no real purposes to be looked for in the world around us.

At the same time, Larkin insists, this world around us is the only world there is. There is very little of a religious sense in Larkin; there is little hope of another world which will redeem or compensate for the shortcomings of this one, and thus we must make the best of what we have. Indeed, for Larkin, there is a strange beauty to be found mysteriously even in the most unexpected places – in the habit-influenced world of the Whitsun weddings, for example, where although he seems to be far removed from the world of uncles shouting smut, 'the perms,/The nylon gloves and jewellery-substitutes', nevertheless even these can provoke in him the sense of the spiritual we get in the last lines, when the train slows

> And as the tightened brakes took hold, there swelled
> A sense of falling, like an arrow-shower
> Sent out of sight, somewhere becoming rain.

We may see this as a further pessimism, since this life-giving rain is not, after all, falling on *us*; yet the pessimism is tempered by a sense that at least happiness might be possible somewhere in the world. And another of Larkin's major themes is this range of mixed emotions which he so frequently describes for us. There is human affection in his poems, but it is often tempered by impatience and a sense of inadequacy; there is sympathy, as for the women in 'Faith Healing', but it is tempered by a sense of the ridiculous. Often alongside all of these feelings there lies a considerable envy of other people, barely concealed in 'Dockery and Son'. This is used ironically in 'Mr Bleaney' where Larkin imagines the life of the previous inhabitant of his own rented room, conjures up for us the presumed pettiness of his life, but ends with two magnificent stanzas where he muses on whether, after all, Bleaney, whoever he was, perhaps understood his own life better than he, Larkin, does:

> But if he stood and watched the frigid wind
> Tousling the clouds, lay on the fusty bed
> Telling himself that this was home, and grinned,
> And shivered, without shaking off the dread
>
> That how we live measures our own nature,
> And at his age having no more to show
> Than one hired box should make him pretty sure
> He warranted no better, I don't know.

Indeed, it is a feature of Larkin's persona that he very rarely does seem to 'know': there is often a hesitancy about his conclusions, an uncertainty as to whether he really understands other people's lives, which reflects on the one hand a kind of humility before the mysteries of humanity and yet on the other a sometimes ironic despair at the impossibility of entering into other people's consciousness.

Larkin, then, is pre-eminently a poet of loneliness and loss. The loneliness is frequently bitter and poignant, as in 'Mr Bleaney'; at other times Larkin is able to make it into a rather painful joke, as when at the end of 'Toads Revisited', in the absence of any other company or solace, he invites the 'old toad' work to be his companion and to 'help' him 'down Cemetery Road' – in other words, to keep him company, at least until the time for death comes.

The loss is not only a personal loss, as we have seen in 'Going, Going'. Larkin speaks, very obliquely, of a vanishing world

> beyond the town,
> There would always be fields and farms,
> Where the village louts could climb
> Such trees as were not cut down

Notice here the highly deliberate selection of the negative word 'louts': one of the most complicated things to grasp about Larkin is the way in which, despite the overriding sense of loss in his poetry, he almost never falls into nostalgia or pastoral. There are exceptions, such as, for instance, 'Cut Grass', which is a short and very beautiful pastoral poem; but in the main Larkin never seems quite sure that even the world which is vanishing would necessarily have been much better than this one. In any case, he might well say, what is the point of wondering about that? That world is 'going' – as, of course, in the pun of the title of 'Church Going' – and all we can do is make the best of the one which seems already to have taken its place, the world of fast profits, free sex and the rule of commerce.

This new world, however, does not have the final word itself, although it may think it does; because – to come on to a final theme of Larkin's poetry – in the end all this new world is trying to do is to cover over the deep unchanging facts of sickness and death, and ultimately it is in his dealings with these inexorable realities that Larkin often seems at his most powerful. The first stanza of 'Ambulances' is typical of this side of Larkin's poetry:

> Closed like confessionals, they thread
> Loud noons of cities, giving back
> None of the glances they absorb.
> Light glossy grey, arms on a plaque,
> They come to rest at any kerb:
> All streets in time are visited.

The image of the 'confessionals' is important, for Larkin often appears to be saying that although death is the end of all things and frequently terrible, nevertheless there is a sense in which we yearn towards it, towards its privacy, as though our death is the one thing we can incontrovertibly call our own, the place where we can at last come face to face with something which is true and which is protected from the debasements of the world outside. Beside this sense of peace, the 'Loud noons of cities' fall back into their proper triviality; the ambulances and all they represent are far stronger than any other force and can afford to ignore the 'glances', and yet they are also intensely commonplace, and sickness and death are all around us, 'at any kerb'; in this image the matter-of-factness of ambulances as road vehicles and their symbolic stature as harbingers of the end of things are marvellously conjoined.

# Form and style

In his mature poems Larkin uses a variety of forms, but we can list a number of features which link his best work together. First, these forms are all quite regular: Larkin is not much interested in free verse, and it is largely in this respect that we can see the influences he received from nineteenth-century poetry and from the tradition of Hardy. He seems not so much rejective of modernism as oblivious to it.

All of his major poems rhyme, and very often Larkin manages to make this rhyming unobtrusive by relying on quite small, unimportant words, and by using a good deal of half-rhyme. Consider, for example, the rhyming words in the first two stanzas of 'The Building': 'hotel', 'see', 'fall', 'century', 'up', 'hall', 'smell', 'cup', 'sit', 'mags', 'bus', 'bags', 'although', 'nurse' – none of these are uncommon words, or words which carry much resonance in themselves.

If, however, we look more closely at 'The Building', we can also see the intricacy of the way in which Larkin builds his rhyme-schemes into his poetry, for the poem consists of nine seven-line stanzas, plus a final separated line – 64 lines in all – whereas the rhyme scheme operates on an *eight*-line scheme of ABCBDCAD. This makes the rhyming less apparent; it acts as a device to carry us unconsciously on from one stanza to the next; it also builds up to the isolation and ambiguity of the separated final line, 'With wasteful, weak, propitiatory flowers', for by the end of the ninth stanza we have a sense that we need this final line to make formal sense of the poem as a whole.

This complicated stanza form is again typical of Larkin's poetry as a whole. He uses lines containing four or five stressed syllables – tetrameters and pentameters – and often stanzas of between four and eight lines; but very few poems are exactly the same. Consider again, for example, 'The Whitsun Weddings', where the run of pentameters is interrupted in each stanza by a second line of two stressed syllables. This is not an accidental feature: this sudden break in each stanza almost before it has begun comes to represent the hesitant movement of the train, which sometimes seems to stop arbitrarily – not in a station, or at the end of a stanza, but in the middle of nowhere.

For a very different example of Larkin's formal mastery, we can look at one of his very few free verse poems, 'Days'. Here there is no rhyme and the lines are all short and appear to conform to no particular syllabic structure. But the poem is held together by certain words – 'days' repeated three times, 'they' also repeated three times (and, of course, an almost-rhyme with 'days'); the 'v' sounds of 'live', 'over', 'live' again, 'solving', 'over' again. This poem also gains a strong effect precisely from the breakage of form: from the sense that the last four lines, 'Ah, solving that question/Brings the priest and the doctor/In their long coats/Running over the fields', do not really fit with the first six, which is itself a deliberate representation of the way in which these people, who are supposed traditionally to bring answers or at least cures to the problems of life, in fact only compound our sense of life's mystery.

But 'Days' is unusual; for the most part, Larkin writes in large, stately, capacious stanzas, and his best poems are probably those in pentameter form – which is the major form of traditional English versification, the preferred form of, for example, Shakespeare and Wordsworth. This line length allows Larkin room to expand his thoughts; but it also allows him to introduce a dialectic, an argument, between the debasement of contemporary life which is so frequently his theme and something grander, larger, more stable.

Thus his use of form becomes in itself part of the argument he is trying to conduct. It stands as a statement that there is a value in tradition: not a value we all have to accept unthinkingly but one which can be recurringly demonstrated in the practice of poetry itself. From our discussion of the themes in Larkin's poetry, it might seem as though his ideas on the contemporary decline of civilisation are similar to those of T. S. Eliot, and to an extent they are; but whereas in Eliot these ideas need to be replicated in a breakdown of traditional forms, Larkin sees such forms as a counterbalance to the surrounding decay. This is not, however, a point he wishes to force upon us; rather he wants it to become clear as we muse on the forms of his verse and observe the way in which he is able to talk about despair and loss *at the same time as* rendering those feelings into well-formed poetry.

The main issue here, however, is to notice the interplay between these traditional forms and the actual styles, the uses of language, which Larkin deploys. If we look again at the opening of 'Going, Going', we can see something of this: 'I thought it would last my time – /The sense that, beyond the town'. These are perfectly formed lines, trimeters in fact, but there is a jauntiness to their rhythm which undercuts any possible sense of formality. Larkin is a master of the art of matching formal versification with the rhythms of everyday speech – in these opening two lines there is nothing which could not occur in an ordinary conversation. We can turn again to the opening stanza of 'Dockery and Son' to follow through this point in greater detail:

'Dockery was junior to you,
Wasn't he?' said the Dean. 'His son's here now.'
Death-suited, visitant, I nod. 'And do
You keep in touch with –' Or remember how
Black-gowned, unbreakfasted, and still half-tight

We used to stand before that desk, to give
'Our version' of 'these incidents last night'?
I try the door of where I used to live:

And then the next stanza begins with the single, isolated word
'Locked'.

This stanza, like almost all the poem, is written in pentameters, but
we notice immediately the break of rhythm in the very first line, the
effect of which is to reinforce the casualness of this opening
conversation (the rhythm is broken only once more, very near the
end of the poem). Within these pentameters, however, Larkin is able
to convey an astonishing variety of discourses. There is the casual
conversation with the Dean. There is the internal description of
'Death-suited, visitant, I nod'. There is the reflective memory. There
is the colloquialism of 'half-tight'. There is the reported, formulaic
speech of 'our version' and 'these incidents last night'. Larkin is able
to make all of these fragments into an intricate weave, held together
by a solid rhythm; perhaps here we see something of the connection
between his poetry and his lifelong interest in jazz, where the
combination of consistent rhythm and the free interplay of different
instruments is all-important.

Larkin's poetry is noted for its colloquialisms, although in fact
there are quite few. In the main, what we find in the poetry is a
determined attempt to represent ordinary speech and the common
processes of thought and feeling. This comes out very strongly in an
extraordinary unfinished poem called 'The Dance', in which Larkin
recounts an encounter at a dance in complicated eleven-line stanzas.
The poem includes these lines:

I face you on the floor, clumsily, as
Something starts up. Your look is challenging
And not especially friendly: everything
I look to for protection – the mock jazz,
The gilt-edged Founder, through the door
The 'running buffet supper' – grows less real.
Suddenly it strikes me you are acting more
Than ever you would put in words; I feel
The impact, open, raw,
Of a tremendous answer banging back

As if I'd asked a question. In the slug
And snarl of music, under cover of
A few permitted movements, you suggest
A whole consenting language, that my chest
Quickens and tightens at, descrying love . . .

Notice first the movement of the very first line, where the notion of clumsiness is so brilliantly underlined by the clumsiness of the line itself, ending as if by accident with the hanging 'as'. Again, the word 'something' suggests a colloquial vagueness, as though Larkin is trying not to dress an experience up in poetic terms thought of later but to recount how the experience was at the time, with all its gaps and uncertainties.

The 'running buffet supper' is of course a colloquial phrase, and one here rendered absurd by its contrast with what is happening to the narrator of this story. When we come to the word 'banging', we sense something quite frequent in Larkin: the way in which he is content to use words which may seem at first glance colloquially inaccurate rather than search for more acceptable equivalents. The point, however, is that by the use of this term, and the 'slug' and 'snarl', he creates a far more vivid impression of the occasion – itself rather cheap and conducive to cheapened emotions – than could be done otherwise. Larkin does not mean to beautify or idealise the experience but to represent, to 'preserve' it, as it was.

No poem, of course, can simply 'preserve' an experience, because the very act of writing and forming implies some kind of change; but another of Larkin's strengths is that, as well as wishing to signal the immediacy of his experience, he is also and often simultaneously able to indicate his inner distance from it; and he does so here in his use of the word 'descrying', which is fascinating in this context, for two reasons. On the one hand, the word means to see from a vast distance and thus signifies a division in Larkin's persona here between the man who is involved in the dance and the man who is compulsively observing it from the outside; on the other, 'descrying' is also a slightly archaic, erudite term which conjures the whole area of the persona's reserved, scholarly being which cannot become fully involved in this seduction.

Thus Larkin's use of form and style often serves to join different realms of experience, in particular, perhaps, precisely this difficult area between the poet's humanity and his being a poet; and it is one of Larkin's major strengths that, as he always wanted to be, he became a poet capable of speaking to an audience to whom these ordinary feelings are familiar without thereby sacrificing the enormous skill and craft he had at his disposal.

# Imagery and symbolism

The difference between an image and a symbol is a puzzling one, and has been explained in many different ways. Principally, it is a question of force. We use imagery all the time: we talk, for example, of someone having a 'sunny' disposition, and we do not mean that literally: we are implicitly comparing the person's temperament to the sun, and in a specific way – we are thinking of the sun as signifying cheerfulness, light rather than dark, warmth rather than cold. At the same time we are necessarily ignoring other attributes of the sun: we do not mean, for example, that the person would make you go blind if you looked steadily at him or her, nor do we mean that the person is millions of miles away from us.

Thus imagery implies selection; and to a large extent, that selection is for us to make. Just so with poetry: a poet will select an image for his or her own purposes. A symbol is a more considerable matter: to refer directly to the sun, or to the moon as Larkin does in 'Dockery and Son', or to a lion or an eagle, is to call upon an already existing range of associations which we can tamper with and use but which are not our property as individuals. We cannot make a lion into a symbol of weakness no matter how hard we try: the cowardly lion in the film *The Wizard of Oz* is precisely a joke about how far we can alter the limits of symbolism.

But in poetry strange things can, and do, happen. Some of the images which poets coin, because of the sheer strength of the language in which they are expressed, attain a kind of symbolic force: they may have a clear purpose, but they also have a halo of mystery which can never be fully explained. The question of whether Larkin was or was not a symbolic poet is one which has occupied many critics, but it need not worry us here; suffice it to say that he was a poet who, like every other poet, used imagery, and sometimes this imagery carried a symbolic force. Here we shall look at four of the most startling images in his poetry and try to see through these images towards the themes we have already discussed.

These four images are: (a) the image of the toads which occurs in 'Toads' and 'Toads Revisited'; (b) the image of the couple in the Arundel tomb; (c) the image of the arrow-shower in 'The Whitsun Weddings'; (d) the image of the high windows in the poem of that name. We have already talked briefly about all of these images in the Summaries above.

The toads, for Larkin, signify ugliness, weight, something which is immovable, and something which continues to exist whether we want it to or not. The very way a real toad sits suggests something which cannot be shifted, something which leads a very different life from our own and which cannot be ignored. This, of course, is what Larkin is saying about what he calls 'work'; but by 'work' he means something broader – the whole burden of habit and routine which exerts power over us. The toads thus signify a limit upon choice. We may think that we choose what kind of life to lead, we may imagine

we are in control of decisions about our own life, career, relationships; but the toads remind us that we are really at the mercy of forces
which we do not totally understand. While we think we are controlling everyday life, it is in fact everyday life which is controlling us.
The toad's purposes are, to us, inscrutable, unintelligible; in the same
way, the patterns which our lives take cannot be fully comprehended
by us. Life is something which happens to us, whether we want it to
or not.

The image of the couple on the Arundel tomb makes a convergent
point, although from a very different perspective. What Larkin is
saying there is that the real couple whose memorial the tomb is could
have had little idea of the future; they would not have known exactly
how they were to be commemorated in stone, but more importantly
they could not even have guessed whether or how their memorial
would survive, still less what people of future generations would
come to make of it.

The connection between the 'Toads' poems and 'An Arundel
Tomb' is that we are again seeing an image of the lack of real control
we have over our own lives, and even over our deaths and what might
happen to our names and our reputations after we are gone. The
difference is that whereas the toads signify a kind of brute ugliness,
the image of the couple is, at least from one angle, a thing of beauty.
What Larkin is therefore saying is that even art – here the art of the
sculptor, but by implication also the art of the writer, of the
poet – signifies an aspect of the lack of control the individual really
exerts over his or her own life.

The arrow-shower in 'The Whitsun Weddings' relates closely to
these other images. We cannot know, Larkin says, where this arrow-
shower will land; in other words, we cannot know what effect our
lives and our perceptions will have on other people. This is similar,
again, to the issue of poetry: a poet may write with one thing in mind,
but when his or her book is read it might be that it produces effects
which are quite different. In the case of 'The Whitsun Weddings' it
seems also as though he is saying something more than this. The
weddings themselves, as he portrays them, are not events with a great
deal of intrinsic beauty: they are ritualised, formalised; the people
who participate in them do not possess much of what is generally
regarded as good taste. Nevertheless in the mind of the persona of
the poem, and for reasons which he cannot fully explain, they seem to
represent a sort of hope.

This reflects something which matters greatly to Larkin, which is
that if we cannot find some echo of beauty among the common rituals
and forms of our culture, then we cannot find it anywhere. Even the
toads have something to reveal; but what is revealed by the toads, by

the Arundel couple, by the arrow-shower, is that we can find hope and beauty only by relinquishing our perpetual anxious wish to be in control of our own destiny. We must realise and even embrace the limitations which are ours because we are human; we must not look to a more perfect, a more ordered or a less fearful world to save us from the present one, but instead we must learn to live in the present with all the tolerance of imperfection and muddle which such living demands.

Thus Larkin's own imagery reflects something of what was said above: namely that the image which attains to symbolic force does so only by accepting that, at the end of the day, there is something mysterious and inexplicable which we have to tolerate and live with, even if this means that we also have an ever-present sense of disappointment. Much of Larkin's imagery, then, relates to ways of living with this disappointment: not exulting in it, nor trying to sweep it under the carpet, but accepting it as part of the texture of our everyday lives.

We can connect the 'high windows' with this body of imagery, for the high windows simultaneously represent the imagining of a better, freer life and the impossibility of breaking through the 'window' to inhabit that better life – except, perhaps, at the moment of death. The high windows are mysterious: does our occasional awareness of freedom relieve us from the tedium of our everyday lot, or does it throw our existence into a terrible relief and reinforce our discontent? Larkin does not answer this question, and his refusal to answer it is enormously important. Poetry is poetry and not another thing because it does not answer questions, because it recognises that at a very deep level the most serious questions are not answerable.

The image, then, or the symbol stands 'in place of an answer'. At the deeper levels of our personalities, in those realms which are revealed in dreams, we do not find answers, nor do we find clearly defined categories or oppositions. We all know the experience when we have, for example, dreamed of a beast and have woken up remembering it as a lion. But when we come to try to describe it to somebody, we realise that in fact it had wings, our mother's eyes, and it spoke to us. The beast of which we dreamed was not clearly one thing or another: it was compounded of bits and pieces; it included contradictions in its very makeup.

This is the case with poetry, and particularly with poetic imagery; and this, of course, is the basis of the reason why the study of poetry is not easy. It is not easy for us to understand or to live with images which seem contradictory, as do the arrow-shower and the high windows; but this is also precisely why poetry is so important, because it shows us a world within us where easy answers are not to be found. It demands not our acquiescence, our agreement, but our imaginative participation.

So these are some of Larkin's key images, and, as has been suggested, they can be related to some of the major preoccupations and themes of his poetry. The question that remains, of course, is how are we to deal with this? How are we to read, study and write about matters which, although we might be able to describe them technically, nevertheless continue to seem elusive?

Part 4

# Hints for study

## How to read poetry

Poetry is not like any other form of writing. It is not designed to be accepted as fact, like scientific reporting or journalism. Neither is it there primarily to tell a story, although some poems, including some of the ones by Larkin discussed above, do tell stories. It is designed to engage not merely the rational, factual part of our mind, nor that part of our mind which is curious to know outcomes and conclusions. You cannot hurry the reading of poetry, for to read successfully demands that you allow your mind, your feelings, your imagination, all to have some free space in which to engage with the poetry.

You will therefore need to read poems several times before you begin to glimpse some of their deeper levels. At first reading, certain images or themes may stand out. Note these down, and make sure they are not forgotten; but then try to cleanse your mind of them before you read a poem a second time. On that occasion, you may find that quite different things stand out; these should also be noted down, and so on through, perhaps, three or four readings, preferably at least a day apart. Do not worry if you find that some of the points you have noted down on different occasions appear to conflict with each other; contradiction and paradox is essential to poetry, and some of the very best critics have made their livings by discovering how contradictory some of the very best poetry is.

Always try to include in your notes some comment, however brief, on how the poem has affected you: what kind of state of mind you find the poem produces in you – cheerful, melancholy, nostalgic, hopeful – for these feelings not only matter to you, but they may also provide you with valuable hints as to the overall mood or tone of the poem. You may well find that a single poem affects you differently at different times: this is the mark of a good poem, and you should note this also and try to speculate on how the poet has produced this variety of potential effects.

Many people are put off by the technical side of poetry – rules of versification, formal metrics and so on. Do not worry about these at first, but try to obtain a basic knowledge of the simpler rhythms. The reason for this is twofold: first, these details of form have also been crucial to the poet him or herself – if you have ever tried to write a poem, you will know how difficult initial choice of form can be, even if you have eventually decided to write in free verse. Second, the technical language of metrics is useful because it is economical: poetry is complicated to describe, and if you can immediately perceive that a poem is written in, say, iambic pentameter, then to say this is far quicker than any other way of describing the form.

The strength of poetry is that it operates directly between two poles: on the one hand, it is the most strongly felt form of writing, and the kind which is most likely to produce strong immediate feelings in you, even if these feelings are not at first particularly clear; on the other hand, it is the most formally complex and tight-knit form, and thus demands great technical expertise. The good reader of poetry is able to apply his or her mind to the technicalities, to appreciate the significant features of form, while at the same time holding on to the feelings. This is not easy, and nobody should pretend that it is; but it offers enormous rewards.

# Organising your work

Almost all poetry should be read aloud. In the case of a lot of older poetry, this was its primary mode anyway: poetry was there to be recited or read and to be shared in communal situations. This is no longer so clearly the case, but it remains true that there is no better way to come quickly to an understanding of the devices which hold a poem together – rhyme most obviously, but also features of rhythm – than by hearing it.

Many modern poets have made tapes of their work; you should always try to find these tapes, perhaps in your local library or through your school. It should be remembered that poets are sometimes eccentric readers of their own poetry: T. S. Eliot is notorious for reading his poetry in the most unattractive way imaginable. Nevertheless there is nothing quite like hearing a poet reading their own work, for at the very least they are going unwittingly to emphasise patterns in the poem which mattered to its creator, whether these impress you or not.

Get other people to read the poem to you. Your teacher will probably organise this in the ordinary course of classroom work; but it is also always useful to pester your friends and relations until they read it to you – and, of course, you can also read it to them and ask what they think of it – or better, perhaps, ask what comes into their minds as they hear it read. A good poem has many different readings, exactly as a good piece of music, classical or popular, can be interpreted in a number of different ways.

Read aloud to yourself. This may initially seem weird or embarrassing, or both; but it is no more strange than singing in the bath, and a great number of people do that. Try to *live* with the poem or poems: sometimes even with a poem you do not initially like or admire (often two quite different things) you will still find that something stands out, a particular phrase, maybe, or a particular verse or image. Sometimes these stand out because they seem to relate to something in your own experience; sometimes they stand out because they are strange and you cannot understand them; sometimes you simply do not know why they stand out. This last case is vital: you should not give up on the 'why', but try out possibilities. Is it that you are reminded of something? Is it that they connect with something else you have read, no matter how unlikely the connection?

It is often useful to keep a 'private' notebook, alongside the notes you are keeping for school or college purposes. There you can note down thoughts and connections which you cannot at the moment justify or explain; you can make sure they are not lost, and the time may well come when you *will* be able to explain them, or at least be able to gain a deeper insight into them. There is no such thing as a definitive reading of a poem: a good poem has a life of its own, and changes before your eyes.

Because poetry is highly technical, it demands a systematic response: in your 'official' notes make lists, use headings (themes, imagery, style, etc.); better still make diagrams which try to relate different parts of the poem, or which relate different poems by the same poet to each other, or which relate one poet's work to another's. Because poetry is designed to excite deep feelings, it demands also a personal response: in your 'private' notes encourage and add to the life of the poem by writing down your feelings, your responses, your related moods; often, even, your dreams can help.

# Writing an examination essay

From what has been said, you will have seen that reading a poem and organising your work around it can generate a great deal of thinking and note-writing. But an examination essay is actually quite short. You will never be able to cram into it even a tenth of what you actually feel or want to say about a poem, or a group of poems, or a poet. It is necessary to keep this in mind, otherwise you may despair.

A question on an examination paper is exactly what it says it is: a question. And a question requires an answer. It does not require a complete assessment of the works of, for instance, Larkin; nor does it require a total assessment of the influences on his works or the context within which he wrote; nor does it require you to claim to have responded to, or understood, the work in question in ways which you have not done. It requires that you attempt to answer the question as you would any other, 'real-life' question: accurately, as far as you are able, and honestly, in terms of your own understanding of the subject. If you were to ask somebody the time and that person were to go into an enormous preamble about how a watch works, or the phases of the moon, or the history of calendars, you would understandably become a little irritated; markers of examinations are often in the position of having to hear hundreds of answers to their carefully worded questions, many of which seem quite determined to ignore the question as set. Try to be one of the few who answer the question directly, clearly, and with evidence for all the principal points you want to make.

There is no getting away from the fact that this requires fairly rapid thinking; after all, no matter how extensively you have perused previous examination papers, you still cannot be sure what the question is going to be, and it is crucial that you do not misread the question – for example, because you concentrate only on the quotation used and forget to study the words of the question itself carefully enough. But you must not panic. Set aside some time – perhaps a fifth to a quarter of the time allowed for your answer – to study the question with due care, to appreciate the points it is trying to make, and to make out a plan of your answer.

This plan should have two basic features. It should list the points you want to make, and it should direct you to the references you want to make to the poetry. Usually these references will consist of quotations, and quotation is demanded in examinations about poetry; but these quotations need not be lengthy – indeed, it is better if they are not – and provided you have enough quoted material it is always possible to supplement this with material requiring less direct quotation. For example, if you have genuinely clinched a point by quoting from poem X, to add that one can find the same thing in poems Y and Z is no bad strategy, even if the time and space for quotation is not available. Even better would be to be able to say which lines in poems Y and Z are relevant.

Most questions in everyday life require a pretty short answer: the examination answer, although short in comparison to what you might have to say about a poet, is long compared with a standard conversational answer. It is therefore important to let your examiner know where you are going. To revert to the previous example, it may on occasions be necessary to inform your marker of issues to do with the history of calendars, but at all costs say *why*. Indicate at the beginning of your essay what you intend to do and to what areas of the poet's work you intend to refer. This will provide evidence of your planning, and it will also keep your own mind applied to the matter in hand and prevent you from rushing off down blind alleys.

Be precise about space. If a question asks you to consider a theme in relation to three poems, make sure that the structure of your essay reflects that. If you are shortweight on the third poem, the examiner, who has a naturally suspicious mind, will suspect that you are running out of material. At the end of your answer always provide a brief account, a sentence or two, of where you have got to, and recall the original question.

Remember that the examiner, in accordance with the polarities of poetry described earlier, is interested in two things, and in a balance between them. On the one hand, what is required is a familiar knowledge of the poetry and an awareness of the objective nature of the poems; on the other hand, the examiner will be looking for evidence that you as an individual have appreciated and responded to the poems on a subjective level. There is thus a place in an examination answer for the objective – 'This poem is structured like this' – and for the subjective – 'I find that it does this for me'. The balance is all-important. Again, if asked the time, you must say that it is, for example, ten o'clock; but if you can add that it is also, in your opinion, a rather fine morning, and the nicest (preferably not the nastiest) there has been this week, you will interest your questioner much more, and a genuine exchange of views will appear possible; and this is the sense you have to encourage in your essay.

# Sample questions

1. To what extent would you agree that Philip Larkin's poetry expresses a nostalgia for a vanished, or vanishing, past?
2. Philip Larkin often writes about boredom. How does he succeed in interesting his readers in the portrayal of such a negative mood?
3. With reference to *at least two* poems, discuss how Philip Larkin treats issues of social class.
4. Philip Larkin often writes about illness, ageing and death. Does this, in your view, make him a pessimistic poet? (You may restrict your answer to *one* of these themes, or any combination of them.)
5. Philip Larkin manages to combine in his best poems a strict attention to form with the accurate representation of colloquial, direct speech. Show in *at least two* poems how he does this, and what effects he produces on the reader.
6. In some of his poems, Philip Larkin adopts the persona of the ordinary man in the street. In *at least two* poems, show how he does this, and to what effect.
7. Discuss the treatment of women in Philip Larkin's poems.
8. What, in your view, are Philip Larkin's major skills as a descriptive poet?

9. Looking at *at least two* poems in detail, show how Philip Larkin portrays the 'generation gap'.
10. To what extent does it seem to you fair to describe Philip Larkin as a poet of solitude and isolation?
11. Looking at *at least two* poems in detail, write an essay on Philip Larkin's use of symbols and images.

# Sample answer

6. In some of his poems, Philip Larkin adopts the persona of the ordinary man in the street. In *at least two* poems, show how he does this, and to what effect.

PLAN

| | |
|---|---|
| **Introduction:** | plan of the essay |
| | Larkin as 'man in the street' |
| | tension with his 'poetic skills' |
| **'Church Going':** | the man who wears cycle-clips |
| | the man who knows the meaning of 'pyx' |
| | commonplace language |
| | changes in tone |
| | literary allusions |
| **'Dockery and Son':** | the 'awful pie' |
| | assumptions of normalcy |
| | build-up to a point where the commonplace is left far behind |
| **'Going, Going':** | jaunty rhythms |
| | strong feel for Britain and being British |
| | the 'village louts', the M1, the Business Page |
| | colloquialism |
| | irrational beliefs |
| | use of clichés |
| **Conclusion:** | man in the street only part of the story |
| | problems of datedness |
| | poetry as permanent/of its time |
| | artificiality and common speech |

This essay will examine three poems in detail: they are 'Church Going' from *The Less Deceived*, 'Dockery and Son' from *The Whitsun Weddings* and 'Going, Going' from *High Windows*. Each of these shows a different aspect of Larkin's adoption of the persona of the ordinary man in the street, and in each case his purposes seem to be different. Also, in all three of these poems we can see that this commonplace persona is in tension with a different persona, one which is more educated, more aware of tradition; it is as though the 'man in the street' part of Larkin is also observed by another part of Larkin, the part which is inevitably involved, as a poet, in the shaping of experience into poetic form.

'Church Going' contains what is probably the most memorable example of Larkin claiming to be an ordinary man. The poem describes a visit to a church which is in itself unremarkable – 'Another church', we are told in line three. At the end of the first stanza, Larkin, 'Hatless', takes off his 'cycle-clips in awkward reverence': in other words, the atmosphere of the church seems to call for some reverent response, but in this modern world where men no longer wear hats the cycle-clips are the only sign available.

The persona pronounces himself ignorant about churches:

> From where I stand, the roof looks almost new –
> Cleaned, or restored? Someone would know: I don't.

Until the third stanza we feel as readers that this ignorance is the only proffered stance; but in the seventh line Larkin refers to 'parchment, plate and pyx', and this helps us to realise that there is a distance between the poet and the persona. The poet is representing a debased modern consciousness without fully sharing in it, and he then goes on in very erudite terms to regret the passing, not of churches, but of what churches stand for in the wider terms of the human spirit:

>                it held unspilt
> So long and equably what since is found
> Only in separation – marriage, and birth,
> And death, and thoughts of these . . .

At the end, in some marvellous phrases, Larkin reminds us of all that religion stands for which is rapidly becoming unavailable to the contemporary man in the street:

> A serious house on serious earth it is,
> In whose blent air all our compulsions meet,
> Are recognised, and robed as destinies.

His language here has vastly changed ('blent', 'robed', 'destinies'), and we realise that there is a mutual criticism going on between the thinness of the contemporary spirit and the outdated but still powerful aura of the church, represented in a difference between linguistic registers.

The protagonist of 'Dockery and Son' returns to his old college and is there reminded of somebody he only dimly remembers, if at all, called Dockery. Being told that Dockery's son is now at the college, he speculates at length on the difference between Dockery's presumed life and his own, in which 'To have no son, no wife,/No house or land

still seemed quite natural'. But his speculations are not those of a
philosopher: they are precisely located (they take place on trains as he
is leaving his college town) and they undergo the vicissitudes of
ordinary, not very concentrated thought:

> Well, it just shows
> How much . . . How little . . . Yawning, I suppose
> I fell asleep, waking at the fumes
> And furnace-glares of Sheffield, where I changed,
> And ate an awful pie . . .

In the contrast between the 'lawn' of his college which spreads
'dazzlingly wide' and these 'furnace-glares' there is a hint of a contrast
between heaven and hell; but Larkin's point is that such elevated
contrasts are always at the mercy of contingency: falling asleep, having
to eat British Rail food.

As with 'Church Going', the tone of 'Dockery and Son' becomes
more elevated as the poem goes on, reflecting a characteristic
movement in Larkin's poetry from simple description through to more
general and abstract thought, but there is a significant moment near
the end:

> Life is first boredom, then fear.
> Whether or not we use it, it goes . . .

The significance of this is that Larkin is now talking about very
pessimistic reflections, but he chooses to do so in a jaunty rhythm
which breaks the more regular iambic pentameters of which the rest of
the poem is formed. This signifies the way in which the consciousness
of the man in the street returns to criticise implicitly the grandeur of the
poetic conclusion: the power of cliché despite the efforts of thought to
transcend it.

The title of 'Going, Going' is a pun: it means that the traditional
landscape of England is disappearing under the weight of new
transport systems, pollution, litter, and at the same time it represents
the auctioneer's chant, so that we are brought to perceive the
countryside and traditional ways of life being knocked down under the
auctioneer's hammer. The voice of the man in the street is evident
throughout in the rhythms, and also particularly in the language of
certain parts, for example:

> The crowd
> Is young in the M1 café;
> Their kids are screaming for more –
> More houses, more parking allowed,
> More caravan sites, more pay.

The question raised here is about how sympathetic or otherwise Larkin feels towards these people who, after all, are victims of increasing commercialisation. This problem is similar to the one which occurs in 'Faith Healing', from *The Whitsun Weddings*, where, referring to women influenced by the power of the faith healer, he says 'Moustached in flowered frocks they shake'. Larkin seems capable of seeing the point of view of ordinary people while not treating them especially kindly, which makes us always unsure quite how he is using their language. Later in 'Going, Going', he says:

For the first time I feel somehow
That it isn't going to last,

That before I snuff it, the whole
Boiling will be bricked in
Except for the tourist parts –
First slum of Europe: a role
It won't be so hard to win,
With a cast of crooks and tarts.

Here there are two separate features of Larkin's language. There is the ordinary slang of 'snuff it' and 'boiling' and there is the exaggerated disgust of 'slum' and 'crooks and tarts'. This makes a reader unsure how far Larkin really understood the man in the street, or how far he used this persona as a vehicle for his own anger.

In general, then, it seems that the persona of the man in the street is only part of the story. Larkin believed that poetry should be the property of the people, and could only really be written about popular concerns; but there are problems with this. If you write about specific details of society, as with the product names he uses in 'The Large Cool Store', then there is the risk of becoming dated. There is the risk of writing a poem which cannot survive its time. Also, in writing poetry, there is obviously a need to make common speech into something more artificial, more heightened, more concentrated.

At his best, as in the three poems chosen, Larkin seems wonderfully able to voice the feelings of the common man while at the same time implicitly criticising how impoverished that speech has become. Perhaps a useful comparison would be with Wordsworth, who also wanted to use plain speech and also commented frequently on immediate social problems, like the decay of the countryside; and since the specificity of Wordsworth's comments does not seem to have detracted from his status as a great poet, perhaps we can hope that the same will be true for Larkin, and that the arguments and conclusions of his poems will gain strength from their use of the commonplace rather than losing relevance because of it.

# Part 5

# Suggestions for further reading

## The poetry

THWAITE, ANTHONY (ED.): *Philip Larkin: Collected Poems*, The Marvell Press and Faber & Faber, London, 1988.
*The North Ship*, Fortune Press, London, 1945.
*The Less Deceived*, The Marvell Press, London, 1955.
*The Whitsun Weddings*, Faber & Faber, London, 1964.
*High Windows*, Faber & Faber, London, 1971.

## Other works by Larkin

*Jill*, Fortune Press, London, 1946.
*A Girl in Winter*, Faber & Faber, London, 1947.
*All What Jazz: A Record Diary 1961–68*, Faber & Faber, London, 1970.
*Required Writing: Miscellaneous Pieces 1955–82*, Faber & Faber, London, 1983.

## Biographical and critical studies

BROWNJOHN, ALAN: *Philip Larkin*, Writers and their Work Series, Longman for the British Council, London, 1975.
COOKSON, LINDA, and LOUGHREY, BRYAN (EDS): *Critical Essays on Philip Larkin: The Poems*, Longman, London, 1989.
DAY, ROGER: *Larkin*, Open University Coursebook, Open University Press, Milton Keynes, 1987.
HARTLEY, GEORGE (ED.): *Philip Larkin 1922–1985: A Tribute*, The Marvell Press, London, 1988.
MARTIN, BRUCE K.: *Philip Larkin*, Twayne, Boston, Mass., 1978.
MOTION, ANDREW: *Philip Larkin*, Methuen, London, 1982.
SALWAK, DALE (ED.): *Philip Larkin: The Man and His Work*, University of Iowa Press, London, 1989.
TIMMS, DAVID: *Philip Larkin*, Oliver & Boyd, Edinburgh, 1973.

# The author of these notes

DAVID PUNTER has worked at the University of East Anglia; as Head of English at the Chinese University of Hong Kong, where he remains a Fellow of Shaw College; and is now Professor of English Studies at the University of Stirling. His published works include *The Literature of Terror* (1980); *Romanticism and Ideology* (1981); *The Hidden Script* (1985); *Introduction to Contemporary Cultural Studies* (1986); *The Romantic Unconscious* (1989); and two collections of poetry, as well as numerous essays and articles on literature from the eighteenth century to the present day. He is currently preparing the New Casebook on Blake, and beginning work on a critical monograph to be called *Passion: a Literary Study*.

# THE MONSTERS' GUIDE TO CHOOSING A PET

Born in Liverpool, Roger McGough has been
captivating children with his accessible, exciting and
witty poetry for more than three decades. In 2004 he
was awarded a CBE for his services to poetry.

Brian Patten is also from Liverpool and one
of Britain's best-loved poets. He is an extremely
popular performer of his work and writes
children's plays and stories, as well as poetry.

## Books by ROger McGough

*Poetry*
ALL THE BEST
BAD, BAD CATS
THE BEE'S KNEES
GOOD ENOUGH TO EAT
AN IMAGINARY MENAGERIE
LUCKY
THE MONSTERS' GUIDE TO CHOOSING A PET
(with Brian Patten)
NAILING THE SHADOW
PILLOW TALK
SKY IN THE PIE
YOU TELL ME (with Michael Rosen)

100 BEST POEMS FOR CHILDREN (Ed.)

*Picture books*
WHAT ON EARTH?

## Books by Brian Patten

*Poetry*
GARGLING WITH JELLY
JUGGLING WITH GERBILS
THE MONSTERS' GUIDE TO CHOOSING A PET
(with Roger McGough)
THAWING FROZEN FROGS
THE UTTER NUTTERS

THE PUFFIN BOOK OF 20TH CENTURY
CHILDREN'S VERSE (Ed.)
THE PUFFIN BOOK OF UTTERLY
BRILLIANT POETRY (Ed.)

*Picture books*
BEN'S MAGIC TELESCOPE